GOLF ARCHITECTURE
IN AMERICA

THIRD GREEN, 184 YARDS, PINE VALLEY, N. J.

GOLF
ARCHITECTURE
in AMERICA

Its Strategy and Construction

By

GEO. C. THOMAS, Jr.

LOS ANGELES
The TIMES-MIRROR *Press*
1927

DEDICATION

TO THE MEN EAST AND WEST
WITH WHOM I HAVE WORKED IN
BUILDING GOLF COURSES, I DEDI-
CATE THIS BOOK.

G. C. T., Jr.

FOREWORD

There are not enough good golf architects for the tremendous amount of golf construction under way and to be developed during the next few years.

Therefore, there is decided need for a book on the practical side of such work, which should be valuable not only to Construction Committees but to beginners among professional golf architects.

There was a time in our golf building when we had no background—when the last word came from abroad; but that time has passed, for even as our players have improved and shown their abilities in foreign competition, so also have our courses advanced in character and diversity.

We now have our own history, our own traditions, our own superlative courses; and on account of our different climatic requirements and topographical peculiarities, we need our own technique added to the general rules of standard usage which we have assimilated from our friends across the sea.

In taking this position, we should revere the cradle of golf with its fine spirit and distinct atmosphere; but we may also be proud of our own development, and strive not only to keep up the standards of our past, but to go on and improve our newer productions, for the ultimate in golf and golf architecture is not yet attained.

In this book it has been aimed to aid the beginner by giving actual experiences in course building, and to place before him the practical working methods found by the writer to constitute sound practice; to illustrate strategy and construction, and to consider all the factors which must be included in the up-to-date proposition.

The present arbitrary values of golf scoring are carefully dissected in connection with golf architecture.

The advantage to be obtained by half strokes for par and half strokes for putter, which has already been suggested by other writers, is consolidated to a conclusion. This new method would not only make our arbitrary values coincide more closely with golf construction, but would reduce the number of hazards which cause undue hardship to the average player, without losing a high standard for our best golfers.

Furthermore, such changes would make our architecture more logical and less costly.

The chapter on Arbitrary Values is presented as a separate problem, and in no way affects the conclusions and methods advanced for use with our present standards.

G. C. T., Jr.

CONTENTS

ILLUSTRATIONS

PAGE

PAGE

DRAWINGS

PAGE

AN APPRECIATION

The illustrations of this book are made available by the kindly interest of those to whom we have written, and who have presented photographs, drawings and other information.

In the East there was the help of my brother, Leonard M. Thomas, who did everything possible to aid, securing assistance from personal friends at Bar Harbor, Newport and the National. Working with him, my associate, Joseph L. Bailey of Philadelphia, secured all the Pine Valley photographs and many others.

Among professional golf architects a former club mate, A. W. Tillinghast, sent prompt assistance with original drawings and photographs, as did Donald Ross, with both of whom I have had the pleasure of working, and to whom I am indebted for instruction in golf architecture.

Among others who sent drawings and information were The Canadian National Railways, Canadian Golfer, Mr. Charles D. Willson, St. Petersburg, Florida, Golf Illustrated, Country Club and Pacific Golf and Motor, The Fairway and The American Golfer, all of whom aided greatly by their contributions.

In the far West the same gracious cooperation was accorded.

Here in Los Angeles the well-known golf architects, William Watson, William Bell and Max Behr gave every possible answer to my requests.

From northern California my good friend, Robert Hunter, now associated in golf architecture with Dr. Mackenzie of England, forwarded drawings by his talented colleague.

Norman Macbeth, of Los Angeles, the amateur architect who built the well-known Wilshire course, and who has since constructed St. Andrews, which is a "pay-as-you-play" course, also gave assistance.

H. Chandler Egan, of Portland, Oregon, formerly our National amateur champion, and at the present time California amateur champion, and who has been so successful with architectural work, particularly at his very wonderful Oswego course, forwarded photographs. Mr. Murphy, the President of that Club, gave the original of the colored reproduction of his course shown on the paper cover.

My friend, Peter Cooper Bryce, of Santa Barbara, who made my reconstruction of the La Cumbre course of that city possible, sent me a number of photographs and drawings, and aided in other ways. His help always means action and result.

The Los Angeles Country Club, Ojai, Bel-Air, the Los Angeles Athletic Club, Fox Hills and others offered what I required.

The city engineers in charge of Griffith Park, Los Angeles, headed by C. B. Worthen, presented me with beautiful contour maps and drawings of the two Los

Angeles Municipal links, which I designed in 1923 and in 1925.

All those who have pictures represented in this book were very kind in presenting me with the same. It would be impossible to use half of the generous gifts, but for all of them I tender my grateful thanks.

However, it was D. Scott Chisholm, golf editor of the Los Angeles Express, who secured a great number of these photographs, and his interest in this and other matters made the book possible.

Coming to California in 1919 with some knowledge of golf construction as related to new courses when associated with capable architects, and with other experience on various green committees in the East, it was the chance given me in the Golden State which made it possible for me to learn more about golf architecture.

Commencing with the Los Angeles Country Club's reconstructed and new 36-hole course, and working in conjunction with plans by Fowler of England, and in consultation with E. B. Tufts, Chairman of the Green Committee of that Club, and for many years president of the Southern California Golf Association, it has been the confidence shown me in this State to which I owe a great part of my training and experience, for the recommendations accorded me for my first efforts here made other construction possible. It has been the faith and courage of those who entrusted me with the building of their courses, which were as necessary as the later aid of cooperation in illustration.

As I go back over the years of my golf there are many faces which come before me, and they are not alone of those with whom I have constructed courses, for to learn golf architecture one must know golf itself, its companionships, its joys, its sorrows, its battles— one must play golf and love it.

I recall fine, old Sam Heebner, of Philadelphia, former Honorary Treasurer of the U. S. G. A., with whom I built Whitemarsh in Pennsylvania, in 1908— a loyal friend and gentleman, long since gone to a better land.

At Bass Rocks, in Massachusetts, from 1901 to the war, I was associated with as great a golfer and true friend as any man ever boasted — Ned Sargent, of Cincinnati. The remembrance of his friendship remains with me, although he also has "gone on."

In those days I played Myopia and Essex, and Bass Rocks, in Massachusetts, and marveled at the new traps which Horace Leeds, of Myopia, constantly built.

The first course I ever constructed by myself was for a small Club sponsored by William Bullivant, of Marion, Massachusetts. I have often wondered why he trusted me, and admired his sportsmanship in doing so.

I was a member of Pine Valley at the time of its construction. I watched George Crump build it. I grew up with it in golfing knowledge. How we all loved George Crump who made this dream possible and how we all sorrowed when he left us! No matter where I live I will always hold my Pine Valley resident membership.

On the Green Committee of the Philadelphia Cricket Club I aided in the work on their reconstructed course, and in the building of their new Flourtown course, the first being done under the supervision of Donald Ross, the second from the designs of A. W. Tillinghast, both golf architects of the highest class. Before this, and as a member of the Sunnybrook Committee, in Pennsylvania, I was connected in its construction with S. Y. Heebner, Joseph Clark, its President, and the professional architect, Donald Ross.

I always considered Hugh Wilson, of Merion, Pennsylvania, as one of the best of our architects, professional or amateur. He taught me many things at Merion and the Philadelphia Municipal; and when I was building my first California courses, he kindly advised me by letter when I wrote him concerning them. He also was a loyal friend and a fine golfer. Alas, that he did not live for his family, his friends and his golf.

Among those who have asked me to build courses was the late E. D. Libbey, for whom I designed and constructed Ojai, in Ventura County, California. When I told him I could do better work if alone and without interference from committees, the fine, old gentleman left me in charge, arranged the finances and went abroad. He returned when the course was complete, and lived to see Ojai's success in the beautiful valley he loved.

I have had the great privilege of knowing George Duncan, of Scotland, for many years, first meeting him in New Jersey during 1910 when the Spring Lake Golf Club of that State was completing its course. I well remember playing in a match with him and our club professional, William Robinson. Duncan went over our new layout and gave us kindly advice concerning the construction.

In most of my California work I have had William Bell, of Pasadena, in charge of construction, and to him I owe much of the success of what I have done. A fine architect himself, Bell has always been loyal to me. He has gone far and will go further in golf construction. In illustrations and drawings and many other matters I must also thank "Billy" Bell.

It is almost impossible to mention all those who have given me valuable aid, shown me different courses and to whom I am indebted, but among the many is Dr. Harban, of the Columbia Club, of Washington, D. C., a fine amateur architect.

During my years of golf I have had the most pleasant relations with many professional golf players, whose advice and help have been of the greatest benefit to me not only in improving my own golf game but also in matters of golf construction.

The average "pro" knows how to play golf much better than the average amateur. He also knows better about the value of the holes played and, therefore, his opinions on construction matters are generally sound.

Years ago I knew and profited by association with "Willie" Anderson, a wonderfully fine player who won the Open Championship. Since then I have known and liked many "golf pros," among them, "Eddie" Loos, who was a mere lad at Spring Lake in 1910; "Jim" Barnes, at Whitemarsh, and so on through my golf until lately, in California, I have had pleasant association with many of our professionals here, including the men at my home club, the Los Angeles Country Club, where Harry McNamara, "Joe" Norwood and "Vic" Dalberto have done me many kindnesses.

So it has been my fortune to be linked with some of the pioneers of golf architecture in the East; and coming to California later, I have been associated with a number of golf pioneers of the Pacific Slope. To all these friends, past and present, I attribute what little I have been able to accomplish for golf construction. They have given me sweet memories of the past and loyal companionships of the present.

GOLF ARCHITECTURE
IN AMERICA

I

DIFFERENT COURSES

DIFFERENT golf clubs or organizations have varied needs, depending on their number of members, the type of those members, and the uses to which the course will be put, in addition to which there is the very important consideration of the financial situation as it relates to cost and upkeep.

The Municipal course should first of all consider congestion; everything hinges on that, for there is the absolute necessity of getting as great a number of players around the course as is possible between daylight and dark, and those many persons are all hammering golf balls in divers ways both as to length, direction and execution, and, like all golfers, are doing it with implements ill adapted to the purpose. In the opinion of the Municipal greenkeeper, all such impeding obstacles as long grass, traps, hazards, one shot holes, and so forth, are best elsewhere, and there is much truth in his belief.

The Municipal golfer must be greatly admired not only by others of the golf species, but by the average citizen, for the Municipal player is a most ardent devotee. He often starts at daybreak, and when he or she plays, true concentration must be attained if shots are to be made at all.

The first time I visited a Municipal course, I was astounded by the fury of the battle. The place in question was narrow and badly congested for lack of proper acreage, and balls seemed to be going in every direction, while men, women and children were scurrying after them in as many different ways. No one seemed to care what anyone else was doing, any more than you or I would consider the story John Smith tells in the locker room regarding his wonderful score.

The gameness and concentration of those golfers was as fine a test of sportsmanship as I ever saw. Everyone who aspires to concentration should play such a course. There was no nonsense as "Please move your shadow off the line of my putt," or, "Stand still, caddie, while I play this shot"—nothing like that at all. It was an endurance contest, and it was played with perfect indifference to outside influence. I admired those golfers; I realized they were far above me as sportsmen and golfers. When I had the chance to help them build a grass course in place of the "skin" layout they were using, I considered it a great honor; and in connection with that course, you may be sure I believed what the greenkeeper had told me regarding the evils of congestion. Our first one shot hole was placed at No. 9, and it was a hole of 225 yards, so that many who played could drive from the tee without danger of interfering with the putting green.

Some other truths about Municipal courses are— the advisability of making very large greens, if possible, those which have two or even three sections

Photograph by Chisholm.

THIRD, 190 YARDS, OJAI, CALIFORNIA

A semi-punch bowl. Deep ravine at the left and out of bounds at immediate right. The shot is of the most exacting nature.

(Thomas and Bell.)

divided by rolls or different levels, so that one section may be played and others rested; also the practicability of mat tees, for on a Municipal course it is difficult, on account of the tremendous traffic, to care properly for grass tees. This latter is especially true of one shot holes where an iron shot is played. The benefit of dog leg holes with hazards at the angles so that the long player may try for the carry of the hazard, and other golfers have exceptionally large open fairways, is another very important factor. On Municipal links or courses with very large memberships, hills should be avoided, and lakes and other natural hazards, which greatly impede progress of the advancing multitude, should not, as a rule, be used; most certainly, such hazards should be few and far between.

Ground rules for such courses should give every chance for lifting from tree bases or water hazards, and so forth; and in other ways aid the players, many of whom are just commencing and know little of the game. All such courses should avoid everything but optional hazards, and give a free way to the hole for the high handicap golfer.

It is most important for the future of golf in this country that every aid should be given to the building and upkeep of Municipal courses, because such will eventually become of the greatest value to the game, and from them we may expect to produce many of our future great players.

There are really but two types of Country Club links other than the greatly overcrowded proposition,

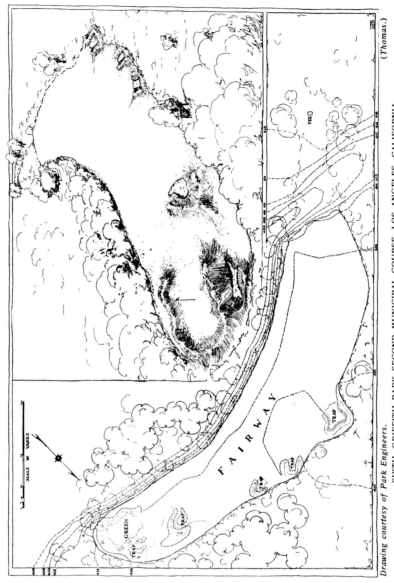

Drawing courtesy of Park Engineers. (Thomas.)

SIXTH, GRIFFITH PARK SECOND MUNICIPAL COURSE, LOS ANGELES, CALIFORNIA.

Fairway built on natural sand.

Photograph by Rau.   *(Macdonald.)*
VIEW ON THE FIFTEENTH HOLE, NATIONAL COURSE, LONG ISLAND.
Francis Ouimet, Christopher Dunphy and Max Marston consider it the finest hole on this famous links.

Courtesy of Country Club Magazine.   *(Watson and Whiting.)*
SEVENTH TEE, HARDING MUNICIPAL COURSE, SAN FRANCISCO, CALIFORNIA.

although, in fact, almost all courses are crowded during rush hours.

The first of these is the Championship course, or, one might say, the Ideal course, and as such must have many things to make it so. It is surprising to find how little the general run of our golfing race realizes this fact.

Once the President of a golf club said to me, "Can you make this the best course in the West?"—and he had not over 100 acres for the eighteen holes with the need of adjacent fairways, if he were to continue squeezing all of them into his limited landscape. When I said, "I could not accomplish this small thing," at once he lost all confidence in me, for to him all was possible, and the man who could not at least promise what he desired was unworthy.

Another time I went over the course of a very select and prominent golf club where they had a beautiful clubhouse placed on the side of a long hill. I walked over the course and saw it was an impossible situation for golf. I tried to be diplomatic and suggested various needed improvements; yet, how could one glory over such a prospect? So, at last, my lack of enthusiasm was noted, and I was asked point-blank for my true opinion of the possibilities. Being cornered, there was nothing to do but speak the truth, and I blurted out, "There are very few possibilities; the ground is unsuited to golf; in fact, it is almost an impossible proposition." Then there ensued a terrible silence.

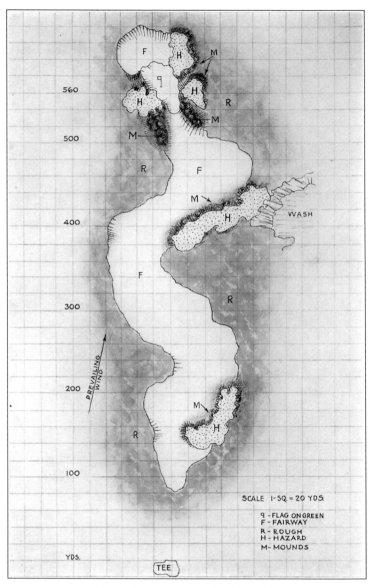

THREE SHOT, IDEAL HOLE, ADAPTED FROM No. 13 FIRST COURSE,
LOS ANGELES MUNICIPAL.

The short player has no trouble if straight, but to secure a par it is usually necessary to
carry driving optional hazard at right. A second trap at right is crossed to reach desired
position which opens the green entrance. Fairway beyond green is an added feature.

Here, again, the love of the golfer for his home came uppermost. That club improved their holes in line with my suggestions, and they play the course as of yore, even though they walk constantly on their side hills. It remains a "horrible" and wonderful creation on account of the topography of the place; but if I motor by, I see them playing, playing, and must admire their love of traditions dear to them. Perhaps I was wrong; perhaps in my idealism I went too far; but, in any event, the course still stands, and who knows but what there are shots on it which I know not of. Yes, it is still there, and mayhap its members secure the same exercise, the same joy of conflict, and the same spirit of the game that others get on finer tests, but, most certainly, such a situation should not be chosen as a site.

In speaking of courses, each man believes that his own is far and away better than most others. He may admit his greens are poor, or that the trap on No. 6 is badly placed, or what not, but, nevertheless, he insists that outside of such minor things, his golf home is superior to most. He brings to mind the niblick shot he played in such and such a match; where else could that have been done? He saw Hagen take a 78 on his course, and no one can prove to him that they have a better layout at so and so. It is remarkable how this holds good. I know one course where there are more blind shots to the greens than at ten other places; yet, do you suppose the men who play that course think it poorer than others? They do not; they think it a fine test, all of which proves that there

NATIONAL GOLF LINKS
OF AMERICA

Self........................ Op'nt........... ....

CHAMPIONSHIP COURSE	REGULAR COURSE	SHORT COURSE	HOLE	PAR	NAME	SELF	OP'T
309	294	290	1	4	Valley		
261	241	228	2	4	Sahara		
410	382	357	3	4	Alps		
185	172	143	4	3	Redan		
478	460	420	5	5	Hog's Back		
130	120	95	6	3	Short		
480	460	410	7	5	St. Andrews		
379	360	296	8	4	Bottle		
542	523	505	9	5	Long		
3174	3012	2744	—	37	OUT		
435	412	371	10	4	Shinnecock		
434	405	383	11	4	Plateau		
397	382	350	12	4	Sebonac		
170	162	125	13	3	Eden		
308	290	290	14	4	Cape		
383	370	350	15	4	Narrows		
419	380	360	16	4	Punchbowl		
315	290	251	17	4	Peconic		
482	460	448	18	5	Home		
3343	3151	2928		36	IN		
6517	6163	5672		73	TOTAL		

Date.................................. Attested..................................

SCORE CARD OF CHAMPIONSHIP COURSE

are many shots in golf, many thrills, the joy of overcoming varied difficulties; and to this is added home loyalty.

So, in considering our Ideal or Championship course, let us remember the value of diversity, and let us include in such a course as many varied shots, and

the surmounting of as many different kinds of difficulties as is possible.

To my mind, the most important thing in the
Championship course is the terrain, because no matter
how skilfully one may lay out the holes and diversify
them, nevertheless one must get the thrill of nature.
She must be big in her mouldings for us to secure the
complete exhilaration and joy of golf. The made
course cannot compete with the natural one; that is
why we so often hear how superior the dunes of linksland are to inland courses, because inland courses are,
many times, uninteresting and flat; but, on the other
hand, there are many inland courses which are as fine
as the linksland by the sea. For example, the rolling
hills of Pine Valley with its lovely contrast of sand
and pine trees and black water, or the romantic mountain country of Ojai with its live oaks and canyons,
surely give us a complete thrill of natural golf, perhaps in transcendent form. So the truly Ideal course
must have natural hazards on a large scale for superlative golf. The puny strivings of the architect do not
quench our thirst for the ultimate, and as part of such
topography we must include sufficient area. Adjacent
fairways do not appear in true Championship layouts.
Each hole should be a thing alone.

Nearly as important as the terrain, is the more
commonplace matter of distances and arrangements.
In this connection we have the writings of various men
to guide us, and the necessary standards are fairly well
established, although, of late, golf architecture has

been considerably improved, and there are changes which add to our courses in the matter of diversity and strategy.

In addition to this, the new golf ball, and the greater distance obtained by it, have helped to change the old order of things.

Generally speaking, there should be two three-shot holes, and of old these necessitated three shots, all of fair length, before the player could reach the green; but, recently, it seems to be more or less accepted that only one of these should be a long three shotter; that is a hole of over 550 yards, because the long three shotter is tiresome. Such a theory may be treason to the old code, but for change and lack of unnecessary length, let us make the other three shotter not much over 500 yards, possibly slightly less. Such a hole gives the long man a chance to get near the green in two, with the possibility of reaching it, and the short man can always attain the distance with three reasonable strokes.

One shotters are most important. In these holes one gets a keener interest on the tee shot than on others, because it may be played to the green by most men. To my mind, five one shotters are not too many. Certainly, a fine test of this type is superior to a poor two shotter, and, in addition, they usually surpass the two shotters in character, because ground for them is easily found, and they may be made with less trouble and expense. Their distances should run from long wood to a mashie niblick, and one shotters on any course

(Crump and Colt.)

FOURTEENTH, 164 YARDS, PINE VALLEY, N. J.

A superlatively beautiful hole from every standpoint, requiring a fine iron shot. Short tee for average player.

				SELF	OP'NT		
YARDS	HOLE	BOGIE	PAR		NAME	SELF	OP'NT

T. SUFFERN TAILER'S OCEAN LINKS
NEWPORT, R.I.

YARDS	HOLE	BOGIE	PAR	NAME	SELF	OP'NT
310	1	4	4	FIFTH AT GARDEN CITY		
545	2	7	6	LONG HOLE, SHORE ACRES, LAKE FOREST		
191	3	4	3	TO THE HARBOR, NORTH BERWICK, REDAN		
305	4	5	4	BRENTON REEF. 1ST NATIONAL		
315	5	5	4	OCEAN DRIVE CAPE HOLE, LIDO.		
140	6	3	3	OCEAN 6TH NATIONAL, 17TH PIPING ROCK		
258	7	5	4	HILL TO CARRY, THEN 11TH ST. ANDREWS		
510	8	6	5	ROAD HOLE, ST. ANDREWS. 8TH PIPING ROCK		
460	9	6	4	RAYNOR'S PRIZE DOG LEG		
3034		45	37	OUT		

A PRIVATE COURSE WHERE A NOTED INVITATION TOURNAMENT OF LOW HANDI-
CAP GOLFERS IS HELD EACH YEAR.

should require not only different types of shots, but different lengths of shots.

Furthermore, by saving ground in the use of one shotters, it is easier to secure better two shotters on the balance of a course, and in badly broken country they help the problem of plan.

The two three shotters and the five one shotters we have arranged will leave us eleven other holes, and these should all be two shotters, and may be roughly divided as follows:

Four long two shotters of from 440 to 475 yards. Two of these should demand full wood to the green, another a spoon, and yet another a cleek or longest iron for perfect play.

Next should come four medium length two shotters, running from 400 to 440 yards, and these should require medium irons, jigger shots, mashie irons, or long mashies, for proper second shots.

The remaining three two shotters must be shorter, and vary from 300 to 375 yards. For the second shot to the green, two of them should demand pitches; one of them a very exacting pitch and run, or running shot. There will be plenty of chance on all holes for short pitches and run ups, and three short two shotters are sufficient.

This would give you a course of the following approximate distances in sequence of yardage:

560	405
525	375
475	350
460	325
450	250
440	220
430	190
425	165
410	145
4175	2425 Total—6600

On a flat piece of land one could balance these holes and have the yardage about the same on both nines, but on most ground this is neither practical nor necessary—other opinions to the contrary—because the greater distances and the harder climbs should be on

Photograph by Meeson.

A GREEN AT ENGINEERS' CLUB, LONG ISLAND.

Courtesy of Devereux Emmet.

(Strong.)

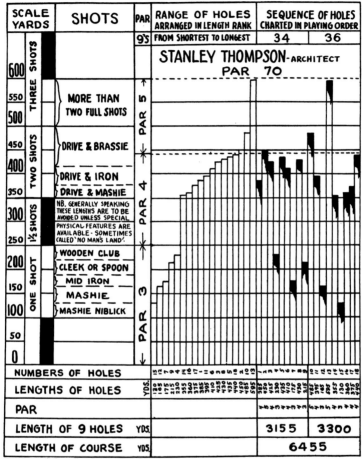

A CLEVER DIAGRAM OF THE JASPER PARK COURSE, CANADA.

the first nine, and the shorter distances and the absence
of climbs on the second nine.

There are many courses of the highest class on
which the nines do not balance, and it is rather a

pleasant prospect than otherwise to feel that the harder part of the course has been overcome after the first nine holes are played. Whereas, when the first nine is rather easy, it is distinctly an objection to have the second nine too difficult.

Furthermore, the skill required on holes of shorter length should be as great as on long holes. Therefore, your ground should decide as to the balancing of your nines, and the shorter nine, as noted, should be second, but the last three holes should be of exceptional character, and the last hole should, undoubtedly, be a fine two shotter.

Where possible, keep the three shot holes in separate nines; place three one shotters on one side, and two on the other; put two of the short two shotters with two one shotters, and the short three shotter on that nine also. If you can do this, you are fortunate.

Could this programme of the distances and the position of the holes be carried out as suggested, the course in sequence of play would read something like this:

460	405
410	325
525	250
220	560
375	190
440	425
145	165
450	430
350	475
3375	3225 Total—6600

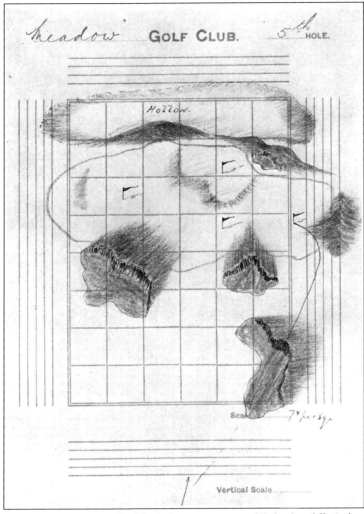

Drawing by Dr. A. Mackenzie of England.   *(Mackenzie and Hunter.)*

Meadow Club, California. 146 yards. Not a copy but very similar to the famous Eden Hole at St. Andrews.

Such an arrangement would give diversity in that no two holes of the same length, and with similar shots to the green, would come together; but such sequence might not be possible on the ground, because many things make it impracticable to arrange distances to suit, and the suggestion is only intended as an ideal, or, as noted before, for a perfectly flat course.

It is advisable to give a good get-away, and not to have a one-shot hole, or a short two shotter, in the first three holes. The writer prefers a hole of 450 to 480 yards as No. 1.

A layout with only four one-shot holes, and therefore one more short two shotter, would generally be considered more logical, but the five one shotters appeal, although the ground naturally decides all such questions, and it is seldom one can do as one desires. It is usually a fight to get sufficient length and to keep out short two-shot holes.

Length means nothing without character, but a true test must have sufficient length and character. Any course with less than two full woods to the green, and two more full woods through the fairways, is lacking in a proper test of wooden club play through the fairway, and all clubs must be brought into use for a complete test.

So much for the first, or ideal, proposition. The remaining type of club course is the short one, with fair to poor character; and no matter what may be said, no test is of true Championship value unless it has proper length, although a short course with character is better than a longer one lacking it.

SUNSET CANYON CLUB, NEAR LOS ANGELES, CALIFORNIA.

A course of nine one-shot holes, ranging in distance from 80 to 200 yards.

(*Watson.*)

Roughly speaking, anything under 6,300 yards is a short course for the present-day golf ball, and unless it has great character, must fall short of the Championship ideal. Such distances mean average ground conditions. A sandy course, where there is little roll, may be longer at 6,200 yards than a clay course in dry weather of 6,500, and other conditions, such as upgrades and prevailing winds, affect yardage. The short course should be trapped, and its strategy should consist of the same principles as the long one. Any club which eliminates character—and character means proper hazards—does not have a golf course in the true meaning of the term.

The hotel course is much on the order of Country Club courses, and need not be considered separately.

In the old days, as has been pointed out by many writers, there were courses where the run-up shot to the green, or the pitch and run, were mostly played. Again the pitch shot was the most frequent one necessary on other noted layouts. Types of hazards differed also, as did the speed of the ground, and courses near the sea had the strong winds of the ocean, and inland breezes were often sneered at in comparison.

Streams and lakes are hazards elsewhere; trees and heavy growth appear in their native districts; rocks cause trouble in other territory; sand dunes are perhaps the ideal hazard, but all hazards may be used for the same purposes, be they railroad tracks, stationmasters' houses, or out of bounds.

Courses which had peculiar characteristics of layout, as noted above, taught the players who frequented them a certain class of shot, and when such a man went to another course, with an entirely different terrain, he found himself at fault, and it was necessary for him to play shots which were new to him.

On the up-to-date course there should be all types of shot.

After all, the various hazards noted above would be of advantage to the player were they all found on one round of golf; and in the up-to-date tests this diversity of hazard and variety of shots are necessary if the new course is to keep up in character with other new courses which are being constructed.

Courses may be very short on account of lack of room, but it would seem advisable that they should be built and developed on the proper theory of strategy; for, while the holes may be of short length, they can be good holes, and made so that there is no undue penalty.

On a very short course, with a small playing membership, additional one-shot holes would give great variety; in fact, on a nine-hole proposition, four of these would supply value and interest; and in connection with one-shot holes, it is generally customary to make these more difficult than if the shots to the green were of approximately the same length as on two shotters.

On a one-shot hole, the starting place is stationary for all, and the problem to be worked out is, therefore, a definite one. For example, if you are making a one-shot hole of 150 yards, it is very different from a

Photograph by Chisholm. (*Byrne.*)
WATER HAZARD AND GREEN ON A 260-YARD HOLE.
Private course of Harold Lloyd, Beverly Hills, California.

Courtesy of Donald Ross. (*Ross.*)
SAND TRAP NEAR CLUBHOUSE, PINEHURST, N. C.

two-shot hole of 350, where the average player should be close to the 200 yard mark, but where, as a matter of fact, everyone drives different distances, and in addition to this, reaches different sides and parts of the fairway. On such a hole, it is not fair to all players to insist on a most exacting shot, whereas on the one shotter of 150 yards, practically everyone can reach the green on the tee shot, and the hole can be made so that a most accurate shot must be played. Therefore, on a short nine-hole course you could secure superlative value by having four one shotters, as noted, rather than short two shotters with more open shots to the green.

On this basis, the idea that very short nine-hole courses are without interest is an erroneous one.

It is possible to make a very short nine-hole approach and pitch course, where the holes will average around 30 yards, all of which will require most skillful playing to secure the average par of 3; and I know of several layouts of this character in crowded districts, which are very interesting and attractive. It would seem that such short pitch and approach courses could be easily installed at many clubs, at hotels, and even for private grounds, and give the utmost pleasure, as well as fine practice, for the short game.*

Furthermore, it is quite possible, on large estates, or any place where there is no chance of much congestion, to lay out two or three greens which can be

---

*For plan of eighteen one-shot holes, or miniature course, see insert following Page 342.

played to from different tees placed so that each tee will supply a different shot to the green; and under this condition there would only be a small amount of fairway required. Such a proposition is advised as supplying good golf and little expense in the upkeep. In such a situation, most of the holes would work out best as one shotters, in which case it would seem only necessary to have one, or, at most, two complete fairways.

Courses with sand greens seem to be on the wane, except in certain portions of the Eastern South, and where, under hot conditions, the water supply is insufficient.

Donald Ross has been very successful with his Pinehurst courses, and the golf there is so attractive that where it is impossible to supply good grass greens, sand greens, based on Pinehurst construction, would be far better. The sand green course requires the same strategy from the tee as one with grass greens, but the shot to the green itself is a different proposition, because it is almost impossible to play pitch shots of any length to such a sand surface. It is, therefore, generally customary on shots demanding pitches to have the sand green surrounded by a flat surface, which gives sufficient area to hold the ball.

In situations where play is given up to a great extent during a hot summer, and where the rainy season in the winter provides enough water to encourage natural growth on the fairways, the grass surrounding the sand greens will supply a good reception to shots, even if pitched near the green during such season.

In districts with very little water, I have seen landing places provided for the drive, which were grassed and watered, and landing places around the green grassed and watered, the balance of the course, after clearing, being allowed to take care of itself; but under hot, dry conditions on clay land, this is an impossible proposition, because if the ground is not taken care of by seeding and watering, topped shots run tremendous distances on it, and a shot off the line sometimes secures greater distance than if played on the island landing supplied.

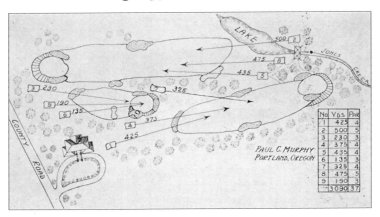

Plan of three greens and fairways with multiple tees which supply nine holes with reasonable diversity.

On the other hand, where there is natural sand, such a proposition would work out very well. You could then make your fairways where you wanted them, and everything else would be a proper hazard, and the ball, which was topped from the tee, would soon lose its momentum.

However, with up-to-date methods, it has been found practical to construct and care for grass greens and fairways in all locations where there is sufficient water supply, natural or artificial. In California the pioneer work which proved this possible was done by Mr. Edward B. Tufts, of Los Angeles.

THIRD GREEN, 238 YARDS. LA CUMBRE, SANTA BARBARA, CALIFORNIA.

(Thomas and Bell.)

II

THE STRATEGY OF GOLF COURSES

THE STRATEGY of the golf course is the soul of the game. The spirit of golf is to dare a hazard, and by negotiating it reap a reward, while he who fears or declines the issue of the carry, has a longer or harder shot for his second, or his second and third on long holes; yet the player who avoids the unwise effort gains advantage over one who tries for more than in him lies, or who fails under the test.

Golf is a game of balance. The man who knows the value of each of his clubs, and who can work out when it is proper to play one and when to play another, succeeds at the game. The ability of a golfer to know his power and accuracy, and to play for what he can accomplish, is a thing which makes his game as perfect as can be; while a thinker who gauges the true value of his shots, and is able to play them well, nearly always defeats an opponent who neglects to consider and properly discount his shortcomings.

As to the clubs themselves, each one has a certain value to the bag, and such an equation has been worked out mathematically by many writers; but it should be noted that one club will be much more valuable with one man than with another, on account of his type of game, his length and his accuracy.

Notwithstanding all these various factors, the putter is, without doubt, the most valuable club in the bag. In a round of par golf the putter should be used not over 36 times, two putts to each green; and if the par of a course is 72 strokes, those made by the putter are half of the total number. If there are four one-shot holes on a course, none of which are of driving length, the driver would be used 14 times, under ordinary conditions, on such a course, and putter and driver together would account for a trifle less than five-sevenths of the total strokes of par. This tremendous total for two clubs shows the great necessity of considering their shots in the most careful manner in the laying out of the various holes. For this reason it is of paramount importance that the tee shots be properly arranged for, because not only will the driver, on the average, be used at least 14 times on most courses, but its starting of the hole gives it further value; for if one starts badly it is often impossible to recover, and, therefore, as a matter of fact, the tee shot bears a greater value than its actual number of strokes would indicate.

The putter, with its par value of 36, as noted above, makes it absolutely necessary that the greens be properly built so that the greatest amount of skill may be insisted upon in the use of this club.

If the putter and driver use up 50 strokes out of the par at 72, this leaves 22 strokes or about two-sevenths of the whole for other clubs after the strokes of the driver and before the strokes of the putter; and the course may be so developed and arranged that these intermediate shots will be played by various clubs, and that different shots with each of those other clubs be demanded by the strategy of the course.

Photograph by Rau.

OPTIONAL CARRY FROM THE TEE AT SIXTEENTH. 428 YARDS. PINE VALLEY.

(Crump and Colt.)

As a matter of fact, the value of these other clubs may slightly increase, because, on the above basis, the hypothesis is that each shot be played correctly, whereas if a man has one weak club and misses the few shots through the fairway which he is required to play with it, the fact that he misses, at once makes this club dangerous in his hands, and increases his score; so that figures as to values of the intermediate clubs are misleading. This is one of the beauties of the game, for just as a chain is no stronger than its weakest link, so no man's golf game can hold together if there is one weak link in his chain of shots, because, when he is called upon to make this shot and fails, his game suffers.

In addition to the shots noted, there are a number of other strokes which a golfer is always called upon to play on account of the failure of his more general efforts of drives and shots from the fairway, and some of the most important of these are brassies after short drives; trouble shots from the rough or from hazards, or difficult lies; and one of the most vital strokes of the game is the short run up shot after a preceding effort which has fallen short or near a green. Such a shot often enables the golfer to place his ball near enough to the hole to go down in a single putt, and thereby recover a stroke which he has apparently lost through a former mistake. All these matters should be considered in the proper building and strategy of a golf course.

There are many glaring errors seen on most of our courses, and one of the commonest mistakes is to have

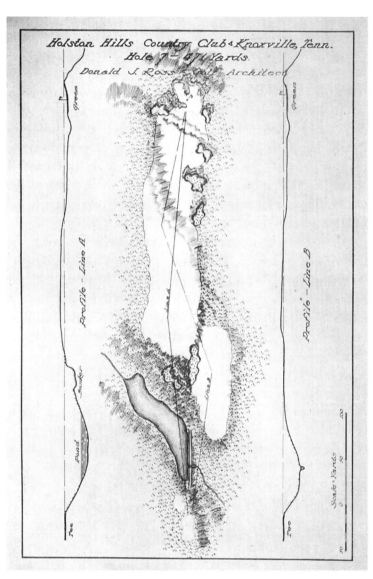

A VERY FINE LONG TWO-SHOT HOLE PROVIDING LINES OF PLAY FOR ALL
CLASSES OF GOLFERS.

a green with a wide opening in front of it, and difficulties nearby, especially beyond the green, or at its far sides; for a man who has fallen short of the green is thereby enabled easily to run his ball up to the pin, whereas the man who has made a bold stroke, possibly lighting on the green with his ball, and running over the green, is given a more difficult lie after a finer effort. To offset this situation, it is advisable in many cases where there are long second shots to a green, to make a fairway beyond the green, so that the man who goes over has at least as good a chance to play back and near the hole as the man who falls short after an indifferent stroke.

Again, this difficulty is overcome to some extent by trapping short of the green, but such hazards must not be too close where a long shot is necessitated, unless there is sufficient room beyond.

Wise is the man who knows how to play each hole as he should play it, and skillful the golfer who can place his shots after he knows where they should go. Such a player is exceedingly hard to defeat on a course with proper strategy.

Where possible, there should be a line of play for every length of golfer, a safe zone which he may try for and expect to reach by his average good shot; but the shorter man, if he dodges the danger of hazards by playing in the open fairway around or short of them, cannot expect to make pars as a rule. Pars are for nearly perfect play, not for puny drives or wild tee shots, unless, after such, the player makes fine recoveries, or holes out in one putt, or by a very ac-

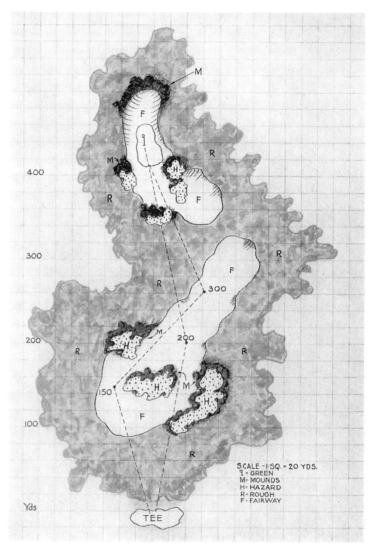

A hole which requires exact placements by short players and fine shots by scratch men, and which provides plenty of fairway beyond green. (From original drawing.)

curate and difficult shot reaches the green after his first ineffectual effort.

On the other hand, hazards should not unduly penalize, and those from which it is very hard to recover are unfair; but the man who finds fault with them is usually a poor golfer, and seldom tries to play backward, or at an angle, if he cannot keep the line.

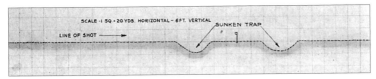

If the green is on flat ground and nothing is raised there is no visibility. Sunken traps do not orient.

But if raised even without sand placed nearby, visibility is helped. Trap could be made short of green to supply earth at back.

Place the golf course on a level plane; have no traps of any kind; let every fairway be flat; the green unprotected and without rolls; let there be no rough; nothing between the tee and the green but perfect fairway, and the green itself absolutely level; and what would be the result?—a thing without interest or beauty, on which there is no thrill of accomplishment which is worth while; a situation untrue to tradition, and apart from the spirit of golf as it was given birth among the rolling sand dunes of Scotland.

Nevertheless, we hear men object to side hill stances, when, if they had played properly, they would

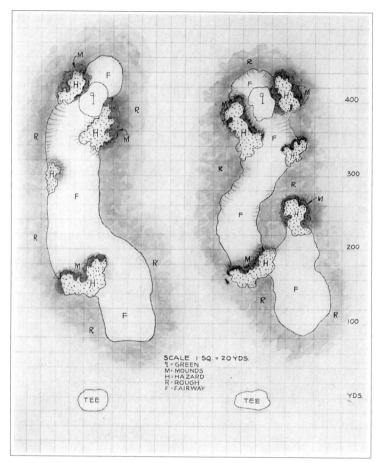

At the left a type of hole often used—the player carrying the left hand trap having a much easier shot to the green, but the short man who goes to the right has practically no chance to try for the pin; a poor hole for the short man, an easy one for the long hitter.

At the right a much fairer hole. The short man has a reasonable chance for the green by going to the right, but the long man cannot play on the same line on account of the trap blocking the way. By taking the left line the hard hitter gets much nearer.

Note fairways beyond—at left for long player, at right for short man. (From original drawing.)

have had a flat lie. We hear them criticise hazards which they claim wear them out with the fatigue of many sand shots, when there was an open pathway which was easily within their powers of attainment. We hear complaints of anything and everything that keeps poorly executed shots, which were played without proper thought, from reaching a situation as advantageous as that secured by another man who has carefully planned and placed his ball.

Those who object to artificial sand overlook the thrill obtained by a splendid recovery, and the variety secured by the use of the trouble club. A number of shots can be played from traps, and these shots are part of golf. Diversify the sand hazards requiring different strokes from them for the best results. On the other hand, too many penalties should be avoided.

Hazards should not be considered as penal, except as they affect the score, and the man who recovers from the artificial peril by a fine shot, not only secures the satisfaction of accomplishment, but learns how to play shots from sand which, on an inland course, he would otherwise know nothing about. There must be enough risk to lend zest to the play, without undue punishment; and, if natural dangers are not present, artificial ones should be constructed.

It is only lately that we have heard of the iniquity of the green with rolls on it; of the error of making any grade on a green which accelerates the speed of the ball after it is putted. In such criticism there is no fairness if the green is condemned when it is undergoing extraordinary conditions. For example, after frost a green may take on speed which it will probably never have at any other time, or in a country where there is generally continued rain and dampness, it will show exceptional pace if there is an unprecedented drought.

As a case in point of such criticism, I well remember an important exhibition match which was played over a new course, when two very well-known golf celebrities were contestants. One of these men was an exceptionally fine putter, having not only most accurate judgment, but a beautiful putting touch. On the greens in question the grass was new; the course had just been opened, and, naturally, the surfaces did not have the turf which, later on, would be attained. When an unseasonable frost condition occurred, the speed of those greens was greatly increased, and, in some cases, it was very difficult to hold the ball on the slippery contours, so that in making a side hill putt more than the usual amount of borrow had to be considered.

One of the men—the fine putter—finished in the low 70s, and the way he handled his approach putts, and the shorter putts, on those treacherous grades was a most beautiful exhibition of skill; in fact, no other part of the exhibition compared to it.

The other man, whose score was not so good, blamed the greens as being too steep. The matter was written about, and the greens were criticised as having too great a grade, and of being too rolling. No one seemed to understand or appreciate the fact of the new grass, and the frosts, which had caused the speed.

(Egan.)

FIFTH GREEN, LAKE OSWEGO, OREGON.
A very attractive double level green, requiring accurate putting.

Courtesy of H. Chandler Egan.

(Macdonald.)

EIGHTH GREEN, NATIONAL COURSE, LONG ISLAND.

Since that time those greens have been improved by increased growth of the grass on their surfaces; and they are one of the features of that course.

The essence of golf strategy is diversity. Greens must be of great variety. One old authority favored different greens having different grasses in order to change the speed as the golfer went from hole to hole, and thereby to acquire an understanding of the different speeds and the ability to regulate the putting touch. This would be logical where some greens were in shade, and, therefore, on account of the retention of moisture, they would be rather slow, while others in direct sunlight all day, especially if they were on high ground which drained easily, would be faster than the shaded greens at low elevation, and which possibly, were on the punch bowl order, and held water. One course I remember which had very sandy soil on one part, and heavy clay elsewhere; and under such conditions this situation of speed is natural and proper. In addition, it has been found that certain grasses do well in shade, and others in very sandy conditions, and so on. Therefore, the thought of the old writer is not ill-timed at this late date.

Yes, the greens should, undoubtedly, have great variety. What interest or sport if they were all flat— all of the same speed; what chance for the real putting touch, and, more important, the ability to judge their speed, their rolls and slopes, so as properly to apply the skillful touch?

The strategy of golf is the thing which gives the short accurate player a chance with a longer hitter who cannot control his direction or distance. It is the factor which permits the brilliant putter the opportunity of recovery; but the flat greens, or the greens with only slight roll, do not supply this interest, for on such nearly everyone is able, as a rule, to go down in two putts, or to hole reasonably long ones.

Under our present values the pars of all holes should require one or two or three perfect shots to the green, according to the length of the hole, and the short two-shot hole should require just as long and as carefully placed a drive to make the second shot possible, as the long two-shot hole demands.

The poorest of all holes are the short two shotters, where a missed first shot allows a recovery to the green that is only a mediocre shot. By reducing the size of the green, by tilting it up from one side to the other, or back or front, so as to require a placement on the drive for a shot which can be played toward the higher part, by making it narrow and long with the opening opposite the carrying trap, it is easy to insist on a fine first shot to make the second one reasonably possible. In other words, if the hole is 300 yards long, and a man misses his drive and goes only 125 yards, he should not be able with an ordinary shot of 175 yards to hope to reach and hold the green. On such a hole the short man, who plays straight, and who properly accomplishes his shot, of 150 to 175 yards, should have a road to the green, through which, by a well-judged and perfectly-placed shot, which is within his ability, he may reach and hold the putting surface.

TENTH GREEN, LOS ANGELES ATHLETIC CLUB.

(*Thomas and Bell.*)

This arrangement is most difficult to accomplish in short two shotters.

The more exacting the test, the more skillful will be the golfers developed; but a really fine test for a long player is likely to make the second shot too penalizing for the short man, especially on short two shotters.

A partial answer to this problem is found by the 300 yard new No. 10 at Los Angeles Athletic Club course, where the green is narrow, yet opens in the line of the short player, but is raised several feet above the adjacent fairway, and with no traps near it. This makes it very difficult for the short man to hold the green; yet he is not punished by traps close by, while the long man must produce a fine second to hold the putting surface unless his drive is an exceptionally long ball.

This practice may be varied on holes of different length by the size and shape and facing angle of the green, and does away with traps. However, it could only be used occasionally, and, therefore, is not a complete solution for the short two shotters.

A variation of this would be to make a punch bowl with all fairway sloping away from it, requiring, as a rule, that the ball be pitched to the bowl, or in a very direct line. Such bowl should be drained at the back.

These arrangements, however, make par very difficult for the average player, but avoid sand recovery.

It is becoming the custom to place two and even three tees on very long holes, or on holes with stiff carries, and does this not answer all arguments as to the length of carries? The back tee is for exhibition matches or scratch tournaments, or for the very low handicap men, and provides a chance to practice for difficult tests of play in tournaments; the middle tee is for general play and handicap competitions; the short tee for beginners or players whose game necessitates its use.

It has been suggested that different players be handicapped by playing from different tees, but this has never been found practical; much better is the plan as explained above.

In connection with tees, where there is a prevailing wind, the regular tee will soon be ascertained, but if the prevailing wind changes to the opposite direction, the value of the hole is at once altered, and the green-keeper should be instructed to use his long tees when there is a following wind, and when there is a very strong, adverse wind, to use the front of his middle tee, or possibly to advance his markers to the most forward starting place. For the same reason, with a heavy cross wind, the markers may be changed, and by such placing of the markers, and the use of the tees, the proper value of course strategy is maintained. From the back tee of a course with several tees, the carry should be from 165 to 190 yards, depending, of course, upon various conditions, such as the prevailing wind and the fact that the hazard may be above the tee, under which condition the distance across the hazard should be reduced. From the center tee the carry should roughly be, under average conditions, from 140 to 165 yards, and from the short tee

120 yards is maximum distance. All measurements should be made from the center of the tee, and where there is a dog leg, the distance of the holes should be taken from the middle of the fairway. The angle of the dog leg should be considered as from 200 to 250 yards, depending on conditions which affect the length of the shot. On some holes there need be no carry from the tee, forced or optional; but here the drive must be placed accurately, and good distance required on it to make the second shot easier or reasonably possible. To develop this theory too far, and omit carries, one would lose diversity; and, in addition, the thrill of seeing your well-hit ball from the tee soar strong and true over a hazard, is a thing not to be too often lost.

In your strategy the wind plays a tremendous part, for it is the ever-changing factor of the course. Where there is a prevailing wind, as a rule, it is advisable to plan your short holes upwind, and, if possible, uphill. It is also advisable to have holes on which the wind comes from the sides, and this has been well illustrated by Braid in his book on Advanced Golf, wherein he suggests as one of the master shots of the game, a man's ability to play for a long slice with the wind from the left, and for a hooked ball with the wind from the right. Under such conditions of wind, the roll of the ground is a most important consideration. If it is necessary to play a shot along a side hill falling away to the right, with an out of bounds on the same side, this should never be played with the wind from the left; and, as a matter of fact, such shot should not be

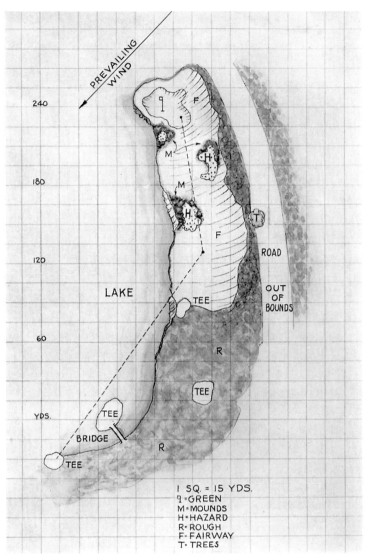

Courtesy of Peter Bryce.   (Thomas and Bell.)

NO. 3, LA CUMBRE, SANTA BARBARA, CALIFORNIA.

Long course, 238 yards; regular course, 214 yards; short tee, 150 yards; back tee (at
left), 320 yards, by dog leg—straight carry 285 yards into wind. Wind almost
ahead slightly from right to left. Ground also slopes the same way.
Four tees give a great diversity of play—the longest one
providing a two-shot hole.

Photograph by Chisholm. *(Thomas and Bell.)*
THIRD GREEN, 238 YARDS, LA CUMBRE, SANTA BARBARA, CALIFORNIA.
Island tee shown at left of center. George Von Elm, Amateur Champion, 1926, standing at far side of green while Harry Cooper putts. (Note drawing of same hole.)

Courtesy of Country Club Magazine.
ON THE COURSE OF THE OAHU COUNTRY CLUB, HONOLULU.

played with the slope to the right, unless it is impossible to work it out some other way. Combinations of the direction of the wind and the slope of the ground provide a great diversity of shots, and add tremendous interest to the play of the holes. For a shot against wind, one may use the pitch to the green, for the wind acts as a cushion, and helps the player to stop the shot; and the green may be greater in width than depth, requiring great accuracy in the distance of the pitch.

Down the prevailing wind, or down hill, give the player, as a rule, the running shot, with a green, narrow in width and great in depth, for the running ball feels the wind but little; and here the architect may insist on direction rather than exact distance.

The green for the running shot may slope away from the line of play, and would make a pitch shot still more difficult on such a hole, enforcing the playing of the stroke desired. This is especially true if mounds which slope away from the shot are built on the green.

In this connection, when a green is planned to receive a pitch shot, there must be no mounds which slope away from the shot, for should the ball on descending hit one of these mounds on its down slope, such shot would shoot or skid dangerously from the mound, and very likely run off the green; but for the running shot such mounds are permissible; in fact, they lend additional strategy. The flat green would eliminate this feature. The principle of the ball skidding from mounds as it descends to the green from a carrying shot applies with even more force to long

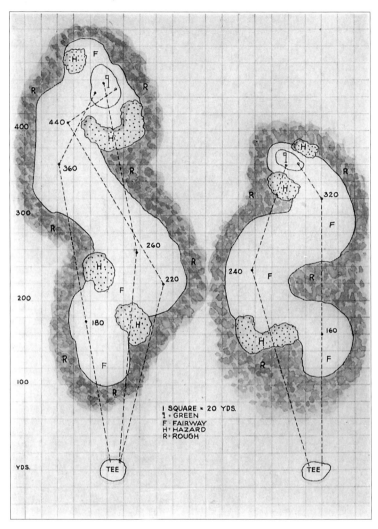

To avoid compulsory carries on second shot of short player, while providing it for long hitter, fairway may be made to right or left of green.

By tilting greens additional strategy may be supplied. (From original drawing.)

(*Bell and Thomas.*)

FIFTH GREEN AT EL CABALLERO, CALIFORNIA.
A pitch hole of merit.

shots than it does to short ones, on account of the added speed of the ball on alighting. Mounds may divide greens, and in such cases they may slope away very gradually from the line of play for pitches, provided the sections of the green are of sufficient size. Rolls are an improvement in dividing large greens into various sections, the size of such divisions depending on the length of the shot to the green, the carry required by it, and the slope of the green itself; for should the green slope away from the shot, it must, of course, be much longer than if it slopes upward from the line of play.

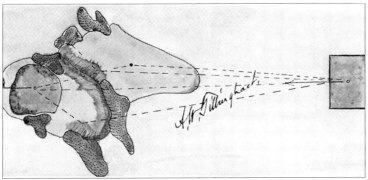

Courtesy The American Golfer.

The Reef Hole, an outstanding type of ridge hazard designed by Tillinghast and described in an article in *The American Golfer* of December, 1926.

Rolls or ridges short of a green are valuable in some cases, but are difficult to cut, and dry out badly in heated conditions. They are only practical in damp climates, unless they may be sprinkled under dry conditions; and one of the most objectionable sights on a golf course is the dried-out mounds and rolls which have not been watered. This applies to all types of rolls, including those which are part of the framework of a hazard.

Nevertheless, rolls with sufficient width for their height, do not dry out easily, and are most interesting as hazards; and in addition to such artificial ridges which affect the course of the ball, natural rolls, or slopes, should be taken advantage of for the same purpose.

A ball hitting on a down slope which slants toward the fairway from either side, will secure a longer run, and, therefore, greater distance—unless the fairways are soggy—than the ball striking the flat fairway. All such runs afford fine strategy, for when the slope is near the rough or traps, the player takes considerable risk in trying to place his ball on it to secure the additional distance, while such traps are out of the way of the short player.

The green with two entrances is very attractive; and one of them may have traps close to it for a short third of the short golfer, and the other entrance have traps further from it for the man who makes a fine carry, and plays a long second for the green. In such case the fairways are divided for the two shots to the green. This is often easily accomplished by rolls or mounds which make more attractive divisions than rough without contour. Holes with double or triple, or even more fairways or landing places, present unlimited possibilities to our golf course development. Such are very feasible, but can only be considered where each hole is separate and apart from the rest

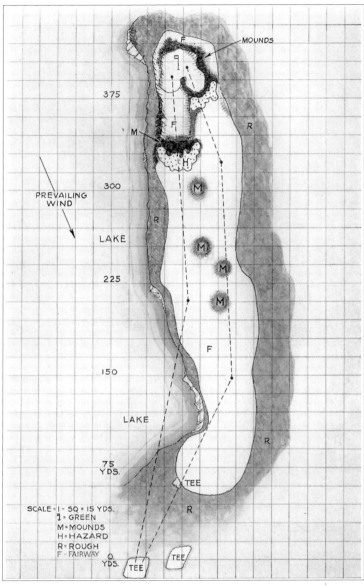

Courtesy of Peter Bryce.   (*Thomas and Bell.*)

NO. 2, LA CUMBRE, SANTA BARBARA, CALIFORNIA.

Long course, 418 yards; regular course, 402 yards; short course, 330 yards. Necessary
to carry lake at left to get a position to play for green opening over left hand
hazard short of green. The short man has a fairway devoid of carries
till his short third and distinct from the long man's fairway
by intervening mounds.

of the course. A green with a central entrance may be trapped with a deep trap on one side, and a shallow trap, where a chip shot will take you out, on the other side; and the player soon learns to keep on the side of the shallow trap. This is valuable where there is a chance of congestion on one side of the green from another fairway, and lack of congestion on the other side; for in such a situation, if the deep trap is placed on a congested side, it forces the players in the desired direction; that is, away from the congestion.

Traps placed at the side of a fairway from which the ground slopes rapidly to much lower levels, protect the shots of the golfer from running down these heavy grades, and are a great advantage also in the quick finding of balls; and especially so when such landing places are blind from where a shot is played. Many situations occur where a trap is a protection from natural hazards, and unless such are near the green, they may be made very wide but shallow, so that the player has a good chance of recovery.

The ability of players to understand the simple strategy of a hole is undoubted, but too often they play blindly and do not consider their best lines. On other holes where the strategy is more involved, the player does not so often discover his best line until he has played the course several times.

Once in a very important Championship, I placed the cup on the left hand narrow side of a small, one-shot green. The shot was a pitch, and near the narrow shelf where the flag waved, there was danger both in front and behind the green; and to hold the ball near

(Thomas.)

SEVENTEENTH GREEN, 120 YARDS, NORTH COURSE, LOS ANGELES COUNTRY CLUB.

The shot comes from the left center of picture. A double level green demanding very accurate play for a par.

(Thomas.)

SEVENTEENTH GREEN, 120 YARDS, NORTH COURSE, LOS ANGELES COUNTRY CLUB.

Picture from in front of green and slightly to left of line of play.

LIDO COUNTRY CLUB

CHAMPIONSHIP COURSE	REGULAR COURSE	SHORT COURSE	Hole	Par	Hcp	NAME	Self	Op'nt		
384	361	335	1	4	9	First				
421	398	364	2	4	7	Plateau				
175	160	142	3	3	17	Eden				
466	505	448	4	5	1	Channel				
378	354	327	5	4	11	Cape				
493	477	458	6	5	5	Dog's Leg				
469	455	438	7	5	3	Hog's Back				
234	175	168	8	3	15	Ocean				
357	334	307	9	4	13	Leven				
3377	3219	2987	—	37	—	OUT				
414	389	360	10	4	10	Alps				
408	393	376	11	4	8	Lagoon				
433	412	386	12	4	4	Punch Bowl				
316	300	283	13	4	14	Knoll				
148	129	107	14	3	18	Short				
404	387	367	15	4	12	Strategy				
206	189	169	16	3	16	Redan				
563	548	528	17	5	2	Long				
424	405	384	18	4	6	Home				
3316	3152	2960	—	35		IN				
6693	6371	5947	—	72		TOTAL				

Self_____ _____
Op'nt_____ _____

Date_____   Attested_____

A course which provides three tee placements. The fourth hole on Lido is considered a remarkably fine test.

the flag required a superlative shot. On the day of this medal round there was a gale of wind from right to left, and the green, which had been in fine condition the evening before, dried out during the night from the strong, dry wind. When the play commenced, there was only one safe line for that hole, which was to pitch to the right of the flag in the widened center of the green, where a shot of ordinary merit would hold. Yet in spite of these danger signals near the pin, man after man in that Championship played straight for it. Only a few thought enough about the speed of the ground to try the center path of safety. As the day advanced, and the wind continued, and many feet tramped the green, it increased in pace, and the difficulties which players encountered on it caused the news of its dangers to spread, until soon a large gallery watched from above the green. The thing became exaggerated. One man, a noted expert, missed his tee shot completely, playing far to the right of the green and behind a large tree. His second was over the green, and he did not reach the putting surface until his fourth effort, after which he four putted the green and totaled an 8. This score was quoted and the slopes of the green blamed for the existing uncommon condition.

As the play continued, very few used their heads on that hole that windy day, for as the news spread, and they heard about the small green and the terrible slope and high scores, and the tricky conditions, the advancing players showed their nervousness very plainly, and the gallery above did not help them.

One man came late. He was a fine, cool, calculating golfer. I watched him rather fearfully, because everyone was finding fault with the sloped green which I had built, and the flag that I had placed. Would this man also fail to play the safe line and ruin his chance to make the winning score, thereby adding

Photograph by Rau.

(Crump and Colt.)

SECOND, 352 YARDS, PINE VALLEY, N. J.

Requiring a forced carry on second shot.

more criticism to a green which was very difficult that day, under most exceptional conditions, but which normally played well?

No! gracefully and confidently he played his pitch close to the center of the green, and then, to make assurance doubly sure, he did not take a chance of over-running the cup with the heavy wind behind his ball, and slipping down the slope beyond. He saw the increasing speed of the green and deliberately short putted on his second, laid his third absolutely stone dead, and then dropped the ball in for a four.

I never admired Macdonald Smith so much as when he proved to that crowd of golfers that the uncommon and tricky conditions existing could be met by the man who played with his head as well as his hands.

On broken ground, hilly ground, or terrain with natural hazards, the golf architect must place his holes so that proper strategy is obtained from the natural topography. On flat, or fairly flat courses, he must place his hazards to take the place of natural ones, thereby attaining his purpose. There are innumerable ways and combinations to obtain this necessary finesse. Some are plainly evident from the tee, others will only be discovered after one plays near the green. Occasionally, your proper line will not become clear to you until you have gone over the hole a number of times. Such problems include the many diversities of carry from the tee, through the fairway and to the green, with the added artifices which may complicate the situation by the size and shape and levels of the green, and the numerous effects secured by dog leg holes, out of bounds, grades, winds, and divers other factors.

Every golfer can improve his game by playing for placement not only on his drive but through the fairway, and by trying to play for the point on the green which makes his putts easier. Years ago it was thought sufficient to play for the green, and if the golfer's shot reached it, he was satisfied. Then men came who played for the flag, and again, if near it, they were content. Now, as the game has developed, the best players try for the proper position near the pin, considering the slope of the ground so that they have the easiest putt, the uphill being easier than the downhill; the putt with the slope above at the right being simpler for most people than if the slope is above at your left, and so on.

Only a few can play wooden shots with enough accuracy for such placement. More people can play full irons skillfully enough for this advantage, and still more can play full mashie or mashie-niblick shots for the same purpose; but practically all golfers can try the short pitch or the short running approach, so that the putts will be easier. Yet, how few try for this simple method of better scoring.

If the average golfer considers the points of strategy which have been worked out in advance for a properly designed golf hole, he will undoubtedly improve his game in his play of such a problem. There is no question but that the strategy of golf is one of its most important assets, and our newer courses present many

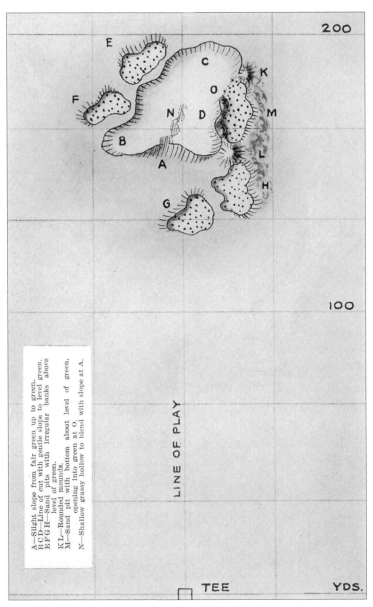

200

100

E

C

K

O

F

N

D

M

B

L

A

H

G

A—Slight slope from fair green up to green.
B C D—Line of cut with gentle slope to level green.
E F G H—Sand pits with irregular banks above
      level of green.
K L—Rounded mounds.
M—Sand pit with bottom about level of green,
      opening into green at O.
N—Shallow grassy hollow to blend with slope at A.

LINE OF PLAY

TEE

YDS.

SEVENTH, 175 YARDS, MOMENCE, ILL.
Reproduced from field note-book of William Watson, Golf Architect. A green requiring
placement.

REPLACE TURF

OJAI VALLEY COUNTRY CLUB

Date

Holes	Yards	Par	Bogey	Hdcp					ALL BARRANCAS ARE WATER HAZARDS
1	520	5	6	1					
2	465	5	5	4					
3	190	3	3	16					
4	400	4	5	10					
5	440	4	5	6					
6	425	4	5	8					
7	410	4	5	9					
8	240	3	4	15					
9	495	5	6	2					
Out	3,585	37	44						
10	450	4	5	5					
11	350	4	4	13					
12	105	3	3	18					
13	320	4	4	14					
14	440	4	5	7					
15	380	4	5	12					
16	390	4	5	11					
17	130	3	3	17					
18	475	5	6	3					
In	3,040	35	40						
Out	3,585	37	44						
Total	6,625	72	84						
Handicaps									
Net									

STYMIE GAUGE

Scorer   Attest

A course requiring placements from the tees.

most interesting situations which increase their value. The question of strategy is of the utmost importance to the golf architect and to the golfer, and such strategy will be developed more and more during the coming years.

III

SOMETHING ABOUT CHOICE AND CONSTRUCTION

I N the two preceding chapters there are many things which pertain to construction; and in this one there must of necessity be matters which concern other subjects, for in all chapters it is a question of overlapping to bring out the full meaning—an interlocking grip of the situation.

A choice of the ground must be considered from the viewpoint of construction, and, therefore, construction and choice go logically together, just as construction and strategy must often be dealt with jointly.

One of the most important considerations in connection with any property is its soil, and we may divide the different kinds into the following classes:

Sandy loam is beyond question the best soil for a golf course. It drains nicely, yet retains moisture; and its capillary attraction is satisfactory. It is easily handled in the development of greens and hazards. It has no fault except that it requires lots of water in a country demanding irrigation. Snow and ice and frost leave it quickly, and it dries out rapidly after rain. The speed of such a course remains more constant during the entire year than any other except pure sand. In fact, sandy loam may be put down as being undoubtedly the best soil.

Pure sand has been made into successful fairways by top dressings of other soil, which include compost. It is possible to use pure sand, or nearly pure sand, but, for even part of a course it is not as desirable in dry, hot districts unless the water supply is amply sufficient. Very sandy soils must generally have sprinkling systems, even in a country with rain during the summer. Pure sand, or nearly pure sand, after treatment, has many of the advantages of sandy loam; and, in addition, its hazards fit most naturally into the surroundings. In fact, it is often unnecessary to make them, as the raw ground supplies perfect ones.

Nevertheless, to have an entire property of natural sand, or nearly pure sand, would entail a tremendous expense in securing top dressing; but where part of a property is of loam, or light clay, from which soil may be secured for the sandy section, it is rather an advantage to have some holes in the property built on sand.

At the Los Angeles Municipal course, several holes on one 18 were made on almost pure sand; and on the second 18 a sandy river bed provided a number of fairways; but good soil was close at hand on the larger part of the property for top dressing.

Pure and heavy clays have disadvantages. They are hard to work, and do not throw off snow and ice and frost quickly; and such soils make for a later opening in the spring in districts with closed winters.

In addition to this, clay needs artificial drainage. It becomes baked, and varies in its speed. On fairways this obtains to a greater extent in countries

Courtesy Hotel Del Monte.   (*Mackenzie and Hunter.*)
TENTH GREEN, 156 YARDS, DUNES COURSE, MONTEREY, CALIFORNIA.
A sandy stretch by the sea.

Courtesy of Canadian National Railways.   (*Thompson.*)
EIGHTEENTH GREEN, JASPER PARK, CANADA.
High mountain country.

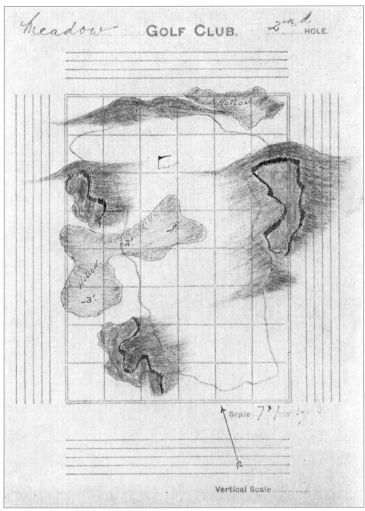

Drawing by Dr. A. Mackenzie, of England.   (*Mackenzie and Hunter.*)

Meadow Club, California. 440 yards. An accurately placed tee shot to the right of the fairway opens up the hole. A pulled drive will present a difficult second.

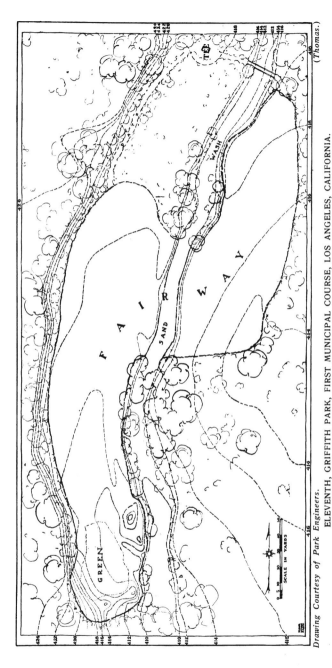

Drawing Courtesy of Park Engineers. (*Thomas.*)

ELEVENTH, GRIFFITH PARK, FIRST MUNICIPAL COURSE, LOS ANGELES, CALIFORNIA.

A double fairway with natural sand as hazard between tee and right-hand fairway. Built in a dry river bed.

without summer irrigation; but in sections where the main course is irrigated in summer, the speed of the ground outside the fairways is greatly increased in a clay soil—a serious objection.

Adobe is a very heavy clay, and it has the additional disadvantage of cracking badly during the dry season. All clays make nasty courses after severe rains, or after too much artificial watering.

Adobe has also the fault of sticking to the shoes of the player during wet weather on any part of the course which is not thoroughly grassed and drained.

In addition to the fact that clay soils are hard to work, construction must cease, if rain comes during operations, which does not hold with a sandy soil. In dry weather very heavy clays, after watering in a hot sun, become much like flint; and this turns the club aside in its down stroke, making play quite difficult. Very often adobe appears in streaks or thin sections running across the course, and under such conditions it may be dealt with by arranging the play so as to avoid such part of the ground for a landing place, and also for greens; but an entire tract of adobe should never be selected.

Gravelly lands, especially with shale or heavy gravel, require extra work in preparing them for seed, but they afford fine drainage; yet they always seem to need the removal of more stones, and those just under the surface spoil many shots. Often these soils must be covered with top dressings after the loose stones are picked, which helps the situation. Here again, the entire property must not be too stony, or the cost of top dressing would be prohibitive.

Districts with many large rocks are usually those with shale or gravel in the soil; and added to these drawbacks there is the additional expense of removing boulders by blasting, or else covering them with heavy layers of soil, so that grass may be grown on them. This is feasible in a damp climate, but it would be almost out of the question in a country where fairways require artificial irrigation. Rocks in the rough are a distinct disadvantage.

Therefore, in the selection of a property, if possible, secure a sandy loam, or at least a light loam, and avoid the heavy clays.

Many golf courses have been built in impossible locations, at additional cost of construction and upkeep.

In connection with soils, it is a question of ease of construction, of supplying drainage, and of ability to grow grass. Any location which gives these requisites is acceptable from the soil standpoint.

Properties will be found which contain deposits of sand. This is very valuable for many uses. Sometimes one finds leaf mould, which is helpful later for dressings of the greens; and, if possible, a tract which has these advantages should be secured.

The terrain is equally important with the soil. Anything from flat land, provided it can be drained, and will not be flooded by overflowing streams, to land without too great hills, may be properly considered golf territory. Heavy hills make the course too weari-

Photograph by Rau. (*Wilson.*)

NINTH GREEN, EAST COURSE, MERION, PA.

A remarkably good one-shotter. Built on a clay loam.

Photograph by Chisholm. (*Thomas.*)

EIGHTH, LOS ANGELES COUNTRY CLUB, NORTH COURSE.

Constructed on very heavy clay.

some, and provide hazards from which it is impossible to recover.

Broadly speaking, where it is necessary to climb more than two steep hills and more than four medium grades, the course is approaching impracticability; and, speaking of hills, those should be considered heavy which require a climb of from 75 to 100 feet or more; a medium grade one which is close to 50 feet. This is a perfectly arbitrary ruling, but is made after a study of the elevations to be surmounted on a number of courses.

In this connection I have just gone over a nine which is somewhat unpopular on account of its hills, and its elevations were roughly as follows:

One hole of something over 300 yards with a climb approximating 100 feet.

A second hole somewhat longer with about a 50-foot climb.

A short hole with a quick climb of slightly less than 50 feet.

In addition, there were several much lighter grades which would ordinarily not be thought of moment.

Therefore, beware of steep hills; but for ordinary grades, and for occasional heavy hills, it is possible to eliminate fatigue by taking them at an angle rather than going straight up the incline. It is also practicable to break a hill by placing a green part way up, and then walking to the next tee up the balance of the hill; for after the rest of putting, the last part of the hill is not so noticeable. On a very long hill divide it with a green, a walk, a tee and a walk. The blind tee shot is better than the long grade.

Sometimes one may make a short climb right or left to a tee, and thereby eliminate part of the hill on the next fairway, for the rest at the tee splits the rise. The worst type of hill is the long, somewhat easy, grade most of the way, with a very steep ascent as one nears the green. Such a hole is also blind, and it is almost impossible to secure good results, on account of this blind feature.

Heavy rolls which come close together are, fortunately, not often found. Where there are low rises, with long, flat spaces between, as in the high sand dune country, they are practical; but land with continuous hills too close together is unsatisfactory for the greater part of the location.

Long, easy undulations with side hills fading into flat meadows, and where there are plateaus or mesa lands, are most attractive. Canyon lands in the foothills of the lower mountains are very beautiful, and offer the added inducement of individual fairways; and individual fairways are of superlative value; for not only does one find splendid strategy in the turns supplied, and in double fairways possible in such canyon or valley country, but, also, these fairways give privacy to the player—he has no interference from other sources.

Where valleys are too narrow, they are not practical. Their sides cannot be properly treated, and where the sides are steep and the space constricted by them, there is always the difficulty of getting to the

Courtesy of William Watson.   *(Watson.)*

SECOND—A ONE-SHOT PITCH.

Lake Arrowhead (5,000 feet altitude), California. Valleys in high mountain country may be used to avoid climbs.

Photograph by Streib.   *(Dunn.)*

LAKE ELSINORE, CALIFORNIA.

Long, fairly easy rolls are very adaptable.

Courtesy of J. Duncan Dunn.

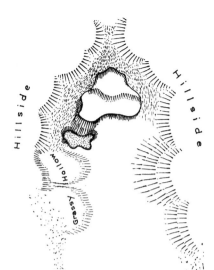

Hillside

Hillside

Grassy Hollow

ELEVENTH, 390 YARDS,
BELVEDERE CLUB,
CHARLEVOIX, MICHIGAN.

. Lies in a miniature canyon with
a grassy hollow behind. The tee
shot should be placed to the left
to ensure an open second. The
green is slightly terraced.

*Drawing by William Watson,
Golf Course Architect.*

LEGEND

 Tees.

 Rough.

 Sand Pits.

 Rounded Mounds.

 Large Grassy Hollows.

 Shallow Grassy Swales
in Greens.

 Slopes.

Hillsides.

Trees.

Tee

next hole, as, often, a steep climb is necessary. In addition, such narrow spaces between low hills drain a considerable area above, as is evidenced by their washes and erosions; and while such make good hazards, they are hard to control in rainy weather. One possibility in this situation is that, as the valleys ascend and one plays up them, it is feasible to cut a path back along the side hill and hold the same, or a slightly higher, level, reaching by such route the top of the hog back lower down, and being able to play into another valley on the other side of the ridge, although sometimes this entails quite a walk.

Therefore, beware of too hilly a country, and only when necessary use the end of a narrow valley shut in by hills.

On a course which I recently built, the clubhouse was placed on the ridge dividing two little valleys, and the ninth green was placed in one of them, and the eighteenth green in the other, at the narrow ends of these little canyons. From the center of the clubhouse above, a shaft was sunk to the level of the greens, and tunnels run from this shaft to the valley close to each green. These tunnels were cemented and lighted, and an elevator in the shaft takes players upward to the clubhouse itself which is near No. 1 and No. 10 tees. Such practice is the exception that proves the rule in the using of hilly country.

The width of a valley or canyon decides if it is wide enough for one, two, or more fairways, with proper space for rough and hazards between. One may figure a fairway at 60 yards as a minimum, with

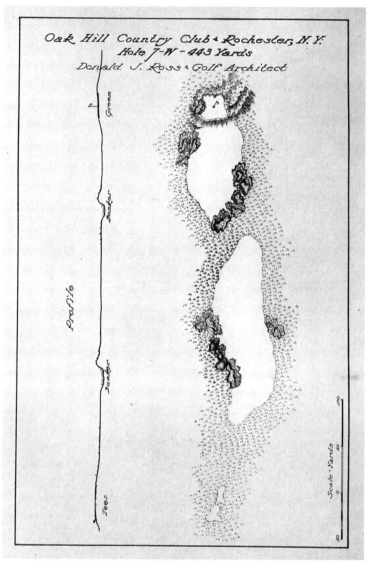

Oak Hill Country Club ⁂ Rochester, N.Y.
Hole 7-W - 443 Yards
Donald J. Ross ⁂ Golf Architect

Clever type of bunkering on a flat hole with segregated fairways.

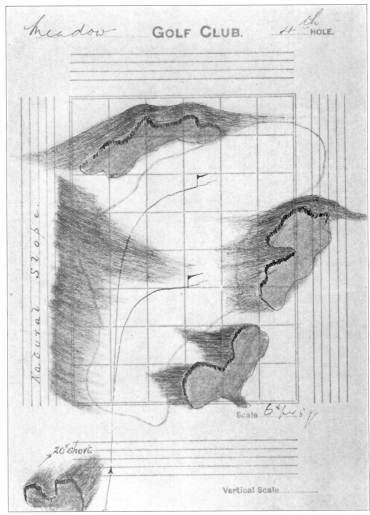

Drawing by Dr. A. Mackenzie, of England.   (*Mackenzie and Hunter.*)

Meadow Club, California. 380 yards. An accurately placed tee shot permits of a run up. A pulled drive will demand a very fine second while a slice will require all carry.

Courtesy Hotel Del Monte. *(Mackenzie and Hunter.)*

TWELFTH GREEN, DUNES COURSE, MONTEREY, CALIFORNIA, 380 YARDS.

Courtesy of Golf Illustrated. *(Barker and Way.)*

THIRTEENTH, MAYFIELD, CLEVELAND, OHIO.

Miss Sterling and Mrs. Hurd in the finals of the Women's National Championship, 1920.

greater width for the dog leg; and there should be at least 30 yards between any two fairways.

In other words, a valley of less than 60 yards in width is too narrow for one fairway, except for the finish of a hole, or a one shotter. A valley of less than 150 yards is too narrow for two fairways to run parallel for any great distance; but it is, nevertheless, possible by the use of a one-shot hole to place them at the ends of valleys of less width for not more than the length of the one shotter. The tee for such a one shotter would be placed on the side of one of the ridges. The ideal valley has 200 yards width, and the holes may go up one side and down the other with plenty of untouched ground between.

Land with trees and wooded country is often used for golf courses. Through such timber fairways may be made individual, and the width be as desired. Such growth often affords protection to nearby tees, fairways and greens.

On one Municipal course young trees were planted where possible in the rough between fairways, and the result was highly satisfactory; but it must be realized that a thin line of trees between fairways is not sufficient to give either protection or character to the course.

While it is expensive to take out woods and build the course where the forest stood, nevertheless it has been done successfully many times. The greatest danger in such work is that of the shade given to the green, which often secures little sun; but this may be overcome by additional tree thinning nearby, which

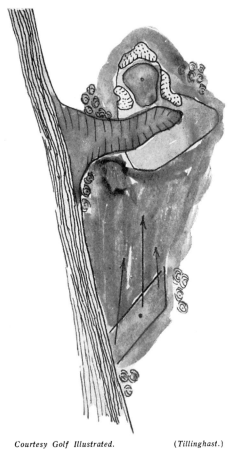

Courtesy Golf Illustrated. (*Tillinghast.*)

The second hole at Poxono, Pennsylvania. Built on the banks of the Delaware—a jigger or half-iron shot.

must be done before seeding, by the use of grasses suitable to shade, and by under drainage to the green, because shaded greens hold moisture too long in all but somewhat sandy soils.

APPROACH TO TWELFTH GREEN, 360 YARDS, BEL-AIR, CALIFORNIA. (*Thomas and Bell.*)

The thirteenth tee is beyond and above—note how green and tee are at the sides of canyon to make room for two fairways.

Fairways, under such conditions, with their rougher grasses, seem to thrive, except in very rocky ground, or where the drainage is bad. In a wooded country one would naturally avoid placing a green on a north slope, because in such a situation it would be more difficult to obtain sunlight. Fairways should be arranged to secure as much sun as possible.

While trees are generally considered poor hazards, nevertheless they may be properly utilized in some cases, but should not be used as carrying hazards. Rather adapt them as impossible carries which must be gone around, often giving a reward for such a play.

Trees and shrubbery beautify the course, and natural growth should never be cut down if it is possible to save it; but he who insists on preserving a tree where it spoils a shot should have nothing to say about golf course construction.

The rough includes all low growth, and it is necessary, but often severe. The lost ball feature of rough is an ever-present evil. Much country will supply its own rough, and the natural is often as good as, or better than, the artificial, and it is adapted to the prevailing climatic conditions; but rough should always be modified, if too heavy, so that it is generally possible to get the ball back on the fairway in a properly executed stroke.

Long grass should not be too long. Other kinds of rough may be thinned here and there. Rocky ground should be picked over and improved; and no rough should be so severe that, as a rule, several strokes must be tried before a player is able to recover, or that recovery is almost impossible. This, of course, does not apply to water hazards, or to canyons in a country without rain, which are treated as water hazards under the rules.

As bad as unfairly severe rough is rough which gives no penalty, the worst type of which is hard, bare ground where the topped ball runs fast and far, and from which it is easy to play a long recovery shot by use of jigger or well-lofted shallow spoon. Such improper rough is often found on clay soil in a country which requires irrigation for its fairways in summer, and where the unwatered land at the side of the fairway has become baked, and is practically without growth. The remedy is the planting of trees staggered along the edge of such rough, with occasional sand traps, and, if possible, watering.

Water hazards are among the best and most thrilling of natural strategy, and sometimes artificial water hazards are well conceived. Like everything else, such trouble should not be overdone. As noted before, diversity, and yet again, variety, is the spice of a golf course. If one could have a course with sand dunes, with water hazards both as streams and as lakes, with fairways through virgin forests, with long, rolling contours, high plateaus, lovely little valleys to play through and to cross as hazards, one would have the superlative and almost ideal golf country. Such is Pine Valley, laid out by the master hand of that sterling sportsman, George Crump. Every true golfer loves Pine Valley. It may be censured by some as very difficult, especially recovery from the rough; yet its charm is the lure of

Photograph by Strohmeyer.   SCARSBORO COUNTRY CLUB, HARTSDALE, NEW YORK.   *(Tillinghast.)*

A swamp where a tee will be constructed. Note corduroy. The fill for green was taken from far hillside. Typical of problems presented at Winged Foot and Fenimore.

Courtesy of A. W. Tillinghast.

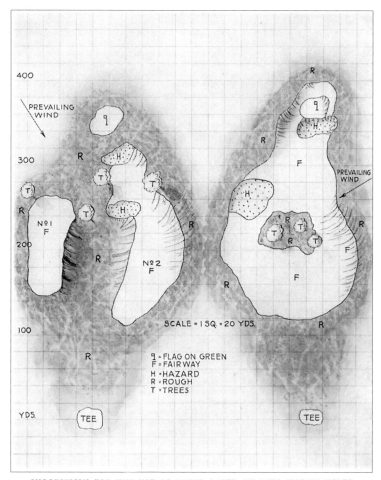

SUGGESTIONS FOR THE USE OF TREES, BASED ON WELL-KNOWN HOLES.

At the left there are trees blocking the way as hazards after badly placed drives. The shot from No. 1 F to the green has good visibility and is on the same level. The shot from R, between fairways, is blind and over fair-sized trees. From No. 2 F the shot is blind and from lower level, but the trees orient the green.

On the right high trees render their carry almost impossible in the center. The long player who places his ball on slope to right of trees secures great length. Any shot played in the center is penalized by trees and rough. The short man, by going to the left, has reasonable chance to reach green on second. (From original drawing.)

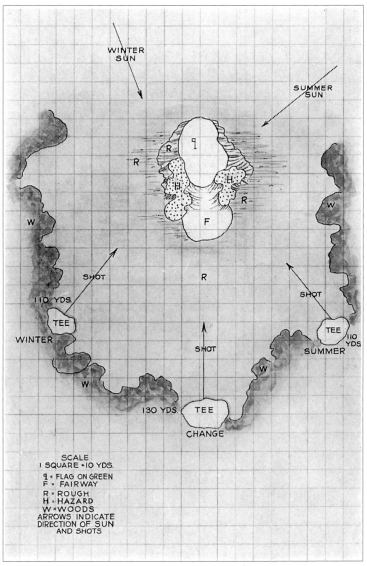

Tees placed to avoid the setting sun while supplying different shots to green. Principle of No. 16, Los Angeles Athletic. (From original drawing.)

diversity coupled with the thrill of surmounting its varied hardships.

Pine Valley is for superlative play. It demands length and accuracy from the tee, and fine field shots for perfect golf. While its heroic carries are in the minority, nevertheless there is not always a safe path for the short player. Its hazards penalize severely, and its strategy compels finesse; but Pine Valley would be impossible for a Municipal course, on account of the congestion which would arise. Its type of topography and construction would not be adaptable to a crowded country club proposition. To my mind, Pine Valley is the acme of golf in this country, and any club which expects to build a fine test of golf should, if possible, have members of its committee carefully inspect Pine Valley.

The outlook of a course as regards the afternoon sun is of the greatest importance. For example, if the property is a long, narrow one, running toward the setting sun during any considerable part of the season of play, it will be readily understood that holes in that direction will be objectionable in the afternoon; and if for some reason the clubhouse must be at the sun end of such a property, the difficulty is prohibitive.

The tract to be purchased must have a clubhouse site where several finishing holes on both nines of an eighteen hole course have the sun at their back. The thirty-six hole layout must also finish away from the setting sun. By noting possibilities for the clubhouse site the avoidance of sun holes as finishes is a simple one.

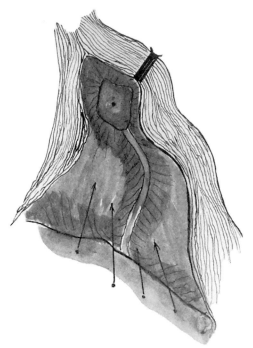

Courtesy Golf Illustrated.   (*Tillinghast.*)

Poxono, Pennsylvania. The green is near the inter-
section of the Delaware and Binniekill. A mashie shot
from a wide teeing ground.

Let us grant that you have found the country for
your course, and that a location has been picked on
which the soil is also satisfactory—the project is ready
for the construction programme. The next step is the
laying out of the course, and often such course has
been laid out in the wrong sense of the term.

Above all things do not start with anyone who has
not done such work before, and done it well, for those

EIGHTEENTH, 425 YARDS, PINE VALLEY, N. J.

A very fine finishing hole with forced carry on second shot.

SIXTEENTH, 367 YARDS,
BELVEDERE CLUB,
CHARLEVOIX, MICHIGAN.

The green is on a high shelf to
the left of the fairway. Its irregular shape demands a careful
approach.

*Drawing by William Watson, Golf
Course Architect.*

Hillside

Tee

LEGEND

 Tees.

 Rough.

Sand Pits

Rounded Mounds

 Large Grassy Hollows.

 Shallow Grassy Swales
in Greens.

 Slopes.

 Hillsides.

 Trees.

of us who have come through the fire of our own errors in golf construction realize how easily mistakes are made.

Many clubs have suffered from experimentation in golf construction.

Because a man has played golf well, has seen many courses, or even because he has, in addition, technical knowledge on other kinds of construction, it does not mean he can construct a golf course properly the first time he tries it.

Today, I finished a trap guarding a green. The membership had just played over it for the first time, and I knew I was in for more or less criticism, because the placing of a trap always causes comment, and it is funny how this often takes an unexpected form. Today, the latest hazard seemed to find some favor, but one man said: "Why do you not lead the ball to the sand by cutting a swale to the trap?" The reason was that the green in question was at the lower end of a little valley; the valley drained quite an area above; in rainy weather the water ran down this valley, and the suggested swale would lead plenty of that water to the trap. So, to offset this danger, we had raised the ground next the trap on the entrance side, and the trap deflected this water from the green below. Not only did that hazard protect the green from badly played golf balls, but it was of practical value; yet probably not one player in a hundred noticed that vital fact.

As important as keeping rain water from running into a hazard and flooding it, is the same danger from the artificial water of the course, because, otherwise, the irrigation will always flood or partly flood a number of traps, even if the greatest care is used by the men at work. In many soils artificial drainage of traps is not necessary, but in clay soils it is absolutely imperative. Traps may be built so that it is possible to drain them. Where it is necessary to put a trap in a flat piece of land, a well may be dug some distance from the trap, filled with loose stone to near the surface, and a drain run from the trap to this well which will take care of ordinary conditions.

The best way is to raise the trap above the fairway level in clay land.

Where hazards are placed near a green, they should be protected from the green water the same as from

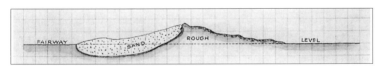

Upper hazard for sandy soil with drainage. Mound made by earth from cut. If water is close to surface in low land of any soil, raise hazard above ground level.

Lower hazard for clay soil without drainage. Mound made from nearest obtainable earth.

fairway water. All such drainage is more necessary with a clay soil, and seldom required where the soil

is fairly sandy or gravelly, unless the situation is in a
pocket.

In placing of traps one must think not only of the
golf value, but also of the drainage, and of many other
things. It takes some years to learn the dangers which
one may run into by the improper building of a trap,

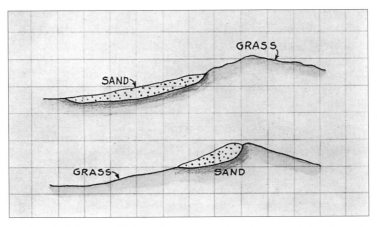

Instead of placing sand below and grass above, why not reverse and place the sand
above where it will orient the shot better, require less sand and never receive water?

and the public wrath which descends upon the heads
of those who make such placements. Therefore, do
not fear to pay the price of a well-known golf architect,
one who has worked at his craft for some years, and
whose best reference is the reputation he has earned
in nearby parts of your own district; for the golf course
in a land of unknown conditions, is an unsolvable
problem to a newcomer. As an example of this, consider the necessary watering of a California course;
and this leads to the important consideration of water
supply.

Even in the East it is found necessary to water many greens and some fairways, and such irrigation will become more prevalent; otherwise, unwatered courses in dry districts will fall into unpopularity.

In California an average eighteen-hole course needs 25 miner inches of water as a minimum during the hottest part of the dry season. 25 inches has 250 gallons a minute flowing steadily all the time.

After you have selected your architect and your location—and the former, if he does not aid in the choosing of the latter, should certainly pass upon it before purchase—you must have a frank and workable arrangement with your architect. This should not only be without possibility of misunderstanding from a business standpoint, but also as to the kind of course most desirable for your needs; the length of your course; the carries from the tees; your club's ideas of the trapping of the greens; of their construction, and other matters most necessary for you to programme in advance—these should be thoroughly discussed and decided upon.

Having talked of different courses, of strategy, and of some construction matters, let us take up more specialized problems of the work itself in the following chapters.

IV

THE GENERAL PLAN FOR THE PROPERTY

THE WELL-CONCEIVED golf property must be designed as a whole; and while it is true that plans of the clubhouse and its necessary adjacent buildings, parking space, and so forth, should be worked out and submitted by the usual experts, nevertheless your golf architect must be consulted as to the situation of such units; for if they are not properly located they conflict with the course itself, and everything can be made to dovetail without interference.

Too often the site for the clubhouse is arbitrarily made, and the golf course must adapt itself to such selection. Many, many clubhouses are situated in locations which hamper the proper laying out of the course, and which are the cause of much discomfort to the playing membership.

One very common error is to place the clubhouse on the highest point of the property, which is often at a corner, making it very difficult to start and finish the course. Again, such a high point is at the end of a long, narrow strip of land, or located at the Western limit of the holdings, so that to return, the golfer must face the setting sun. Much criticism aimed at finishing holes is the fault of the clubhouse location rather than that of the golf architect.

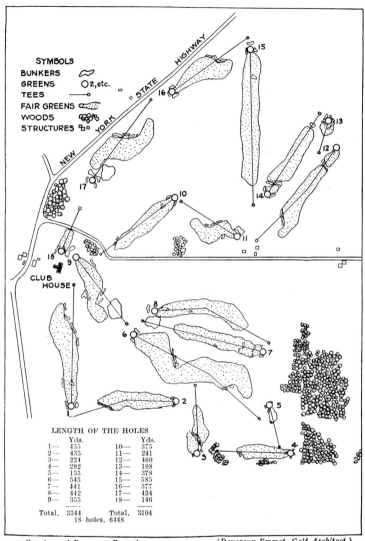

LENGTH OF THE HOLES

	Yds.		Yds.
1—	455	10—	375
2—	435	11—	241
3—	224	12—	460
4—	292	13—	108
5—	155	14—	378
6—	545	15—	585
7—	441	16—	377
8—	442	17—	434
9—	355	18—	146
Total,	3344	Total,	3104
		18 holes,	6448

Courtesy of Devereux Emmet.   (*Devereux Emmet, Golf Architect.*)

McGREGOR LINKS, SARATOGA SPRINGS, N. Y.

Situated in a wonderful country of natural sand. The sixth hole is very fine.

One course which I built had this selected club-house before I started work, and the location was on top of the loftiest hill obtainable. It was especially bad in this instance because on the property there was one little valley of much lower level than the balance of the land. This valley had to be used for several holes on one of the nines, and there was only one practical way to get out of it. After reaching the main level by that outlet, there was room for only one hole from such point to the clubhouse, which, as noted above, was on the very highest elevation.

It was necessary to force the golfer to climb out of the lower valley after he had played his No. 8 or his No. 17, and then compel him to surmount another heavy hill to reach the clubhouse; and owing to other conditions it was imperative that these climbs be placed on the seventeenth and eighteenth holes. The one blot on that course is this uphill finish, and there was an-other clubhouse location which would have avoided the difficulty.

If it is advisable to build on the edge of your property, use the central part of your eastern bound-ary.

There are many advantages in a hillside location, of which the one most often quoted is the view; but this should be secondary to the matters cited above. Where these can be properly handled the hillside is of fine value.

One of the most logical locations for a clubhouse is that of Whitemarsh in Pennsylvania, in the con-struction of which, in 1908, I was the pupil of Samuel

Photograph by Grafton.

CLUBHOUSE AT WHITEMARSH, PENNSYLVANIA.

Heebner, formerly the Honorable Treasurer of the U. S. G. A.; a man who aided in the building of some of the earliest of our Eastern golf courses, and to whom I owe many lessons in construction, in the theory of golf strategy, and in all things pertaining to the fascinating work of golf architecture. Whitemarsh clubhouse faces south, is on that side of a hill which continues to ascend behind the house, giving shelter from the North winds, and there is room for a fairway along the crest of this plateau behind the house. The scene is lovely, and the finishing holes have no discomfort from the setting sun.

The theory that the center of a property is a bad location for the house site is, to my mind, a mistake. I believe the central site is the best location for many reasons. The private roads for approach can be as easily avoided as the public roads which must be close to the clubhouse near the edge of a property, and your private roads used for entrance may be located as desired.

Furthermore, the site near the center of a property gives privacy, and the paramount advantage of returning to the main building with loops of holes, while a site near the edge of a holding makes it almost impossible to secure four nines on a 36-hole layout, and on an 18-hole course, limits your starts and finishes to a very small area.

As important to the course as the clubhouse site, is the entrance for members, the caddie and professional buildings, the arrangements for handling the

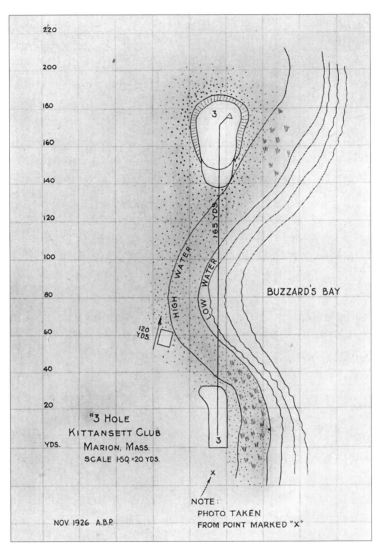

220
200
180
160
140
120
100
80
60
40
20
YDS.

3

HIGH WATER

LOW WATER

165 YDS.

120 YDS.

3

BUZZARD'S BAY

#3 HOLE
KITTANSETT CLUB
MARION, MASS.
SCALE 1 SQ.=20 YDS.

x

NOTE:
PHOTO TAKEN
FROM POINT MARKED "X"

NOV. 1926 A.B.R.

Drawing courtesy of Frederic C. Hood.   *(Wilson, Flynn and Hood.)*

Courtesy of Country Club Magazine.

SPOKANE COUNTRY CLUB, WASHINGTON.

Courtesy of Frederic C. Hood.   (*Wilson, Flynn and Hood.*)

THIRD, KITTANSETT, MARION, MASS.

(Note drawing, Page 123.)

caddies, and all items necessary for the care of the service end of the proposition.

In considering clubhouse locations do not overlook in cold climates the comfort of the southerly exposure with a hill at the back, such situation giving the greatest warmth and protection from North winds in winter, the earliest possibility of enjoying the outdoors in spring, and the coolest breezes in summer. A hillside which slopes to the north is, on the contrary, a bad placement under most conditions; and where there is a shut-in winter, this north slope is the latest part of that district to lose its snow, ice and frost in the spring. The matter of the proper exposure is vital everywhere.

In taking thought to the general plan of the property and the placing of the clubhouse from the golf standpoint, it must be understood that these must not eliminate other very necessary and important factors which concern practicability for the clubhouse. It may often obtain that in the center of a property, or, in fact, in many locations, the clubhouse would lose value, or its surroundings would lose value; and the suggestions made from the golfing standpoint should no more be arbitrary than should the arguments advanced for the placing of the clubhouse be arbitrary; but all these things should be considered together, and the best solution worked out not only for the golf course but for the clubhouse.

Often an old home on a property may be utilized for the clubhouse. Examples of this practice are found at Whitemarsh, and at Sunnybrook in Penn-

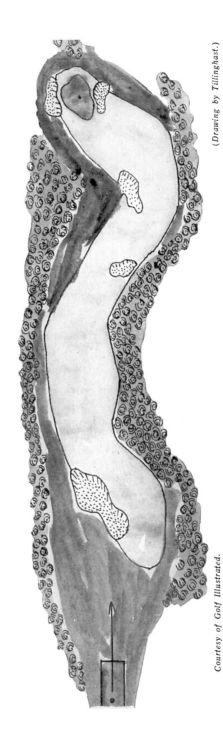

POXONO, PENNSYLVANIA.

An interesting variation of Tillinghast's original Double Dog's Leg.

(Drawing by Tillinghast.)

SECOND GREEN, RED HILL, UPLAND, CALIFORNIA.

(Thomas.)

sylvania. The former built a locker house with an old barn as foundation and walls.

With the buildings placed in conformity with these needs, it should be easy to place 36 holes with four nines starting and finishing near the house, or 18 holes with at least a loop of nine, a loop of six and a loop of three holes starting and returning.

If possible, it is well to have the second hole come back to the club, so that tie matches may for the first three holes be never over the distance of one fairway from home. Also, if one is late in arriving one may pick up friends at the third tee.

For 18 holes this ideal with four tees and four greens near the center of things would give No. 1, No. 3, No. 10 and No. 16 tees as starts, and No. 2, No. 9, No. 15 and No. 18 greens as finishes, or loops of two, or seven, or six, or three holes. No. 15 is suggested as a finishing place, because many matches are over at 14, 15, 16 and 17 greens, and the walk home from 14, 16 and 17 greens would be the distance of but one fairway. Such a plan would also allow the pleasure of continuing for either 2, 3, 5, 6, 7, 8 or 9 holes with a return home to the clubhouse, or near it at the end of such play.

Conditions of topography might easily make such a layout impossible, but most certainly something on the same order would be practical, and its value undoubted.

As noted before, the perfect course should have individual fairways, for not only is it finer because each hole has no interference, but it uses only those contours best suited to its needs, whereas the course which is crowded together cannot choose, and there is always the misfortune of placing some greens and fairways in positions which have disadvantages.

On a flat piece of ground, all of which is available, an 18-hole course of fair to good value may be made on 120 acres as a minimum, on the basis of 6,200 yards for length, with 60 to 65 yards as average fairways. Under these conditions the fairways would require close to 80 acres; tees, walks, waste spaces, 8 acres; rough between fairways at an average width of 20 yards—which would be very narrow for such rough—close to 27 acres. This would leave five acres for the clubhouse, parking space, caddies, and so forth, or a total of 120 acres.

On one hand, very popular courses of fair value have been made on properties of smaller acreage. On the other view of the question, Pine Valley is the choice of many acres. It should always be remembered that a successful golf course increases the value of adjacent land, and that a club, by buying a tract, say of 200 to 300 acres, may readily use the medium and high elevations for the house sites, and the level and lower land for its 18-hole course; and by so doing work the golf course into the contours best adapted for it, letting the holes wind through the tract with individual fairways; and after completing the course, selling the unused portion of the tract. However, for such a scheme a most careful plan must be made at the start, so that space for the roads to the houses put on the sold portion, do not conflict with the play.

(Crump and Colt.)

SEVENTEENTH, 335 YARDS, PINE VALLEY, N. J.

This hole is uphill and plays longer than the given yardage. A very difficult second for the average golfer. A hole with individual fairway.

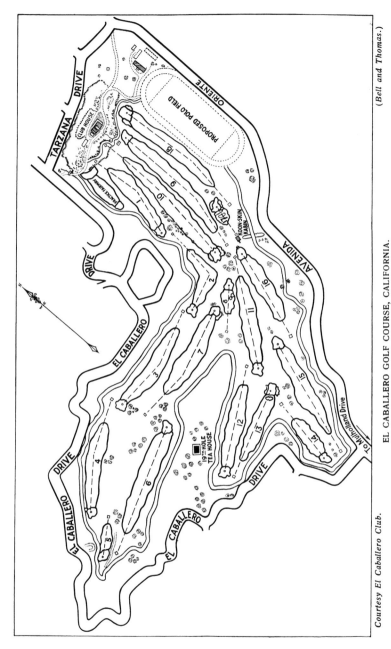

Courtesy El Caballero Club.

EL CABALLERO GOLF COURSE, CALIFORNIA.

A course within a subdivision.

(Bell and Thomas.)

Beware of the man with land to sell who wishes you to build a golf course so that you can sell the land for him. Too often such a proposition brings conflicting interests into being and the course may suffer. Lay out your course first; do not skimp the rough between it and the lots to be sold later and after the course is completed; then, and not until then, build the subdivision.

By such a careful method you will secure the maximum of golf value, use the minimum of land for your course, and develop the largest possible portion for sale without harming your layout.

Do not strive for length where you sacrifice character. Your yardage is the less valuable of the two considerations; but sufficient length, with type and strategy, is the ultimate. The course which demands the greatest number of placements from the tee, and the most diversity of shots, both from tee and to green, is the best test. Far better a fine medium length hole than a poor long one. On the other hand, do not sacrifice length providing no undue local conditions render it impractical; and in selecting the land for your course always look for diversity on different types of ground to be played over.

When you play a course and remember each hole, it has individuality and change. If your mind cannot recall the exact sequence of the holes, that course lacks the great assets of originality and diversity.

(*Thomas and Bell.*)

FIFTH GREEN, 440 YARDS, OJAI, CALIFORNIA.

V

BEAUTY AND UTILITY

IN GOLF construction art and utility meet; both are absolutely vital; one is utterly ruined without the other. On the artistic side there is a theory of construction with a main fundamental that we copy nature; in this all seem to agree. There are minor exceptions which are permitted, as the placing of sand traps in a country otherwise devoid of sand; the cutting of fairway and green with uncut surroundings; the planting of varied trees, shrubs and grasses which do not always blend with existing conditions, and the practical necessity of including fittings and implements required in the general scheme of upkeep and play.

The contours of our tees, of our hazards, of our greens, of our rough and of our fairways should, except when otherwise absolutely necessary, all melt into the land surrounding them, and should appear as having always been present. The washing of water makes smooth, gradually fading lines, as, for example, the sand bar; and the soft, rolling curves of low, gently rounded hills are most attractive if copied in our moulding. Where we have natural washes, many of their lines fade imperceptibly, and float or vanish into other contours with which they come in contact. Such flowing, graceful curves are very valuable in the artificial contouring or modeling of approaches to

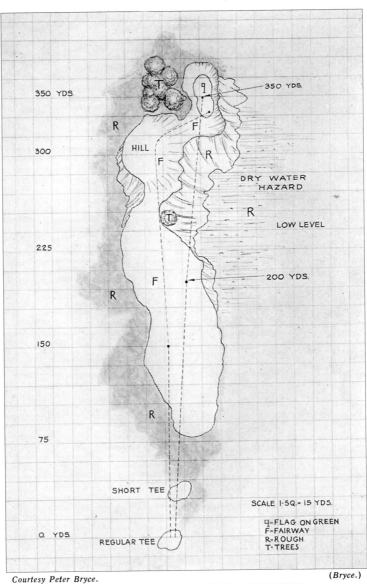

(*Bryce.*)

No. 16, LA CUMBRE, SANTA BARBARA, CALIFORNIA.

A superlative hole requiring placement by both shots of scratch man and giving a reasonable chance for the short player to reach the green or its neighborhood by playing over the hill (line at left). One of the few natural holes of this length where perfect balance is supplied to the long and short players. Strategy masterful; but a very difficult hole for average golfers. Long tee, not shown in cut, increases length to 416 yards. (Illustration of green, Page 143.)

Photograph by Black D.

THIRD, LAKESIDE, HOLLYWOOD, CALIFORNIA.

Note the sand at top of roll. A beautifully moulded approach.

(*Behr.*)

greens, of greens themselves and of mounds adjacent; also for the sides, backs, and fore parts of hazards.

Tees should never obtrude, and, where possible, they may be part of the fairway. Yet, sometimes it is expedient to build them separately, and they should lose themselves, if practicable, as much as other artificial mouldings, into contacting topography.

Raised tees require more water in dry conditions, and are unsightly, but aid utility where, because raised, they give a better view of the shot to be played; and so raised, their boundaries should, of course, fade gradually into the ground near them.

Yet, while easy lines are beautiful and pleasing, they are not the only things we need in our golf architecture from the artistic point of view; and as a matter of utility they are not satisfactory if used alone. Variety must again be considered. We must have a contrast to orient our curving rolls, for not only will it make them prominent, but will aid whatever point we desire in fairway carry or green carry, or green entrance, and most of all of the green itself, to stand out to the view of the golfer. If we blend everything, nothing is accentuated, and in golf the position in which the ball should be placed must be emphasized, and the ability of the player to visualize or focus the distance to such a spot, by aid of our contrasts, is the supreme test of our work. The flat plain, with a flag on a flat green, cannot be oriented, neither can gently blending lines be conspicuous.

For this reason we need sharper and sterner patterns for proper visibility, and we have much in nature to copy. There are the tops of sand dunes gashed by ocean winds, where the sand that once held a curve has slipped away. There are irregular shapes caused by erosion, where water has undermined land, and the overhanging bank presents rough edges amidst the curves. We have hills with jagged slopes, and there are many contrasts in nature made by other forces than those which created the flowing forms, and these have union with our easy rolls.

What better than to imagine our green as the top of some great dune if we desire an island green for a pitch shot; it would give us the graceful arc of the dune, the almost flat top and the broken slant of the sand running down to the level ground below. Sand, under such a condition, gives us variation from the greens color, and here and there a broken part of the dune, caused by slippage, supplies further difference in its harder and severed appearance, and in the shadows it affords.

Again, in fancy, we may leave an entrance between our mounds, and such a gap may be ragged and with shattered outline. Here, perhaps, the green is like a miniature glade surrounded by low hills, and if you will note such country, you will see that its fashion varies. Sometimes the hill is steep, almost approaching the perpendicular, and the lighter cut surface of the green stands out from the miniature hills around it, which have the darker colored grass of uncut rough; this gives us orientation for our golf shot, the dissimilarity of shades of color.

Sometimes trees help by their shadows to throw

SIXTEENTH GREEN, 416 YARDS, LA CUMBRE, SANTA BARBARA, CALIFORNIA.
Shattered outlines supply contrast. (See drawing, Page 138.)

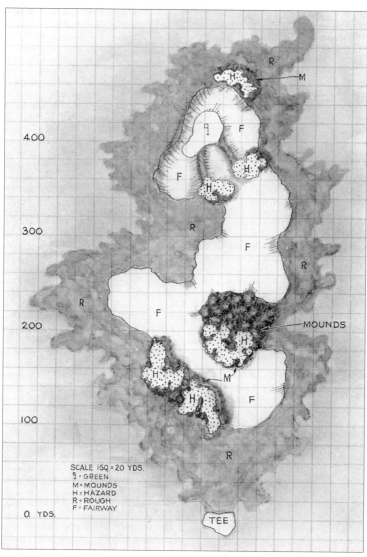

An ideal hole which gives room for the short man to play his regular second and not reach traps short of green. Longer players must make carries from the tee if they wish a par. Mounds and sand back of green help to orient the shot. (From original drawing.)

out a green from its sunlit surroundings, and many other factors aid us in the same way; but often, when we lack these, we turn to the help of the white sand for needed contrast and necessary visibility.

In the surface sketch of the greens themselves we need nothing but the slow, graceful roll, and they may be beautifully moulded in undulations, and hardly ever should these be sharp. Roughly speaking, the peak of any rise on the green itself should have a base at least ten times its altitude. They are easily cut by the mower and do not dry out on top. In the making of these rolls, it is always necessary to have a general plan of drainage, for if you have a sunken valley with no outlet, the water will remain, and underdrainage be requisite.

In the forming of greens, beautiful modeling must conform to what a ball will do when it lands on a green from certain distances, and knowledge of what shot is necessary to reach it from strategetic points, decides the contours of that green.

Rolls must not take up too much of the green. There must be space for the placing of the cup, and plenty of space for its changing; and, as noted, the practical side of green building must consider drainage and subdrainage of the first importance. The green must not hold water; must not be flooded from higher levels, and should be so arranged that it does not drain into traps adjacent to it.

The green ought to be of the proper size for the shot. Its opening for a long shot must have correct width. For short pitches a green need have no open-

Photograph by Bradley.

(*Courtesy Christopher Dunphy.*)

SEVENTEENTH, BAR HARBOR, MAINE.

Considered a very fine hole.

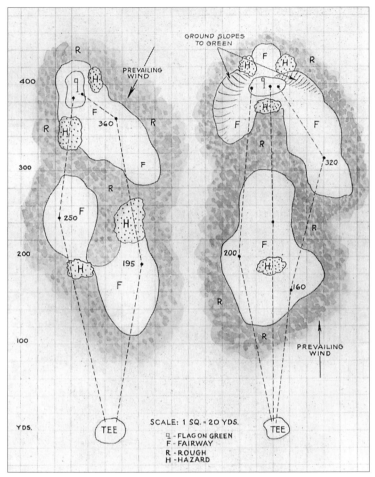

Island fairways which combine fine strategy for both long and short players.
(From original drawing.)

ing for the long player, but the short driver is bound
to have his chance. If there is no opening for the
running shot of the short player, the green must be
larger to hold his carrying shot, and this makes it too

large for the long man's pitch. Therefore, it is advisable, except on very short two-shot holes, to have an opening for the short player, through which he may reach the green with a very carefully executed shot, or else the green must be long for his shot and short in depth for the pitch shot of the long man. This arrangement gives the long man a chance to enter by the short man's pathway, unless provided against. All these matters must be worked out to a nicety, and the strategy of the hole controlled by the angle of the entrance to the green, by traps which control the shots of the short man, and prohibit the long man from taking an undesired line. There are many variations which can be successfully worked out.

Lately it has been found an advance to make fairways beyond the green itself, instead of having mounds or rough behind the green. By placing rolls from 20 to 50 feet beyond the back of the green, one gives a chance for the reasonable return play of the ball which goes over the green; and the mounds a little further back give as much orientation as if closer, while the extra fairway supplies room for the long shot, and reduces the expense of upkeep of large green surfaces.

Such a fairway beyond the green must not be made for very exacting shots, unless you have an opening for the short player which requires a long shot for the green, and on this angle you can give fairway beyond the green; whereas on the line of the long player this fairway should not be made if his shot will be a pitch. This may be accomplished by having a long, narrow green opening up for the shot of the short man on one

Courtesy of D. Scott Chisholm. (Thomas and Bell.)

SIXTEENTH, 390 YARDS, OJAI, CALIFORNIA.

A hole requiring a perfect drive of fine length to open the green to the second shot. Shadows of live oaks orient the green.

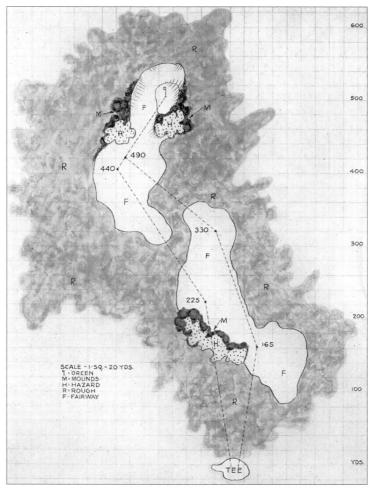

A three-shot hole which is dog-legged to give greater distance, and arranged to make pars harder for the long man, while providing little trouble for average players. (From original drawing.)

side of the fairway, and a trap placed beyond his drive's reach, yet arranged to catch the drive of the long hitter, and which he cannot carry; this will

penalize a topped second shot of the short man. On
the other side of the fairway the long man, by a fine
carry, has his pitch shot to the flag.

Different types of greens are suited to existing
slopes and levels. The shots should, as a rule, play
into the contour; that is, uphill; but this is not always
possible, and has resulted in many horrible grading
atrocities on our golf courses where the green is built
up at the back on down grades. This makes a high
bank at the back, and too often such bank runs almost
straight down to the existing level behind it, an ugly
sight, and one which gives an uninteresting shot to
those who run over. This shot is often very unfair,
unless the green requires a short pitch. It is far easier,

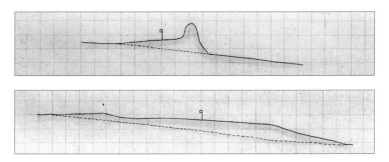

Dotted line, original contour. Solid line, finished levels.

more attractive and less expensive, to make two levels
on ground which slopes away, with an easy running
grade between. However, care must be used in such
a proceeding to be sure the lower green may be seen
by the player approaching it, and, if not, it should be
oriented by higher mounds nearby.

DOUBLE LEVEL GREEN, SUNNYBROOK, PENNA.
A very fine long-iron shot.

PUNCH BOWL GREEN, HUNTINGDON VALLEY, PENNA.
(Green Committee, Smith, Chairman; with advice from Low and Colt.)

Often it will be feasible to provide a running shot for the green which slopes away, and make a very slight rise at the back on such green. Still another plan is to let the green slope to the right or left, and aid the running shot by raising that side of the green which will nurse the ball towards the pin. In other words, if your green curves to the left from the line of play, you can raise the approach on the right hand side, and the ball will run toward the center of the green. By placing a trap short of the green, and immediately in front of it, you not only orient it, but you also penalize the shot which was off the line of its entrance, because, owing to the raised portion, the entrance is to the right of the green itself.

Grass hollows are of good value if they drain easily, or can be made to do so; but those which do not drain are an annoyance. On irrigated land they cause more trouble than elsewhere, unless on sandy soil, because much sprinkling water runs into them and they are generally soggy.

Where there is perfect drainage supplied for grass hollows, and they are watered with care, this soggy condition will not obtain; but usually, with artificial drainage, grass hollows which do not drain naturally, will nearly always cause trouble, and are to be avoided.

At Pine Valley a short two shotter has a green almost at right angles to the line of play, and this slopes away from the properly placed shot, which should be of the running or pitch and run order. The man who cannot place his ball for this shot must pitch over hazards short of the green, and not only have the disadvantage of carrying the hazards, but from the angle from which he plays, his ball will descend on a green sloping somewhat away from his shot, and most likely run off the green.

In this connection it is very difficult to hold a ball with a pitch shot on a green sloping away from the line of play; and while it is advocated by some that such slope should be used to require a shot with extreme cut, nevertheless, it is far better to penalize such a shot, and to give the player a chance for a running shot from another point in the fairway, unless your country is located in a district with much rain, and the green is, consequently, nearly always damp and able to hold the ball.

A green designed for the reception of a pitch shot with a surface sloping away from it, causes extreme penalty to the poor player. If such green be made, it should be of much greater length than the average, to enable the player to hold the shot; and it might almost seem that a little fairway be supplied beyond the green and in the line of play.

Except when necessary for orientation, avoid building greens up at the back, because when the course is properly planned this will be unnecessary, for the shot should nearly always go into the contour.

Where we have a hill to the right, we can make a double level green with a high plateau at the right; and the opposite holds good when the hill is at the left. With high land at the back, it is proper for a

Photograph by Black D.

TENTH GREEN, LAKESIDE, CALIFORNIA.

The running shot played to the right is nursed to the green by the slope.

(Behr.)

green to have two levels with the lower one in front, but in all cases of double levels the total size of the two levels must be much greater than for a single level green. Each compartment must be at least two-thirds as large as a single green for the same type of shot. One of the saddest sights on a golf course is an under-sized double or many-leveled green. To provide the proper playing surface for the reception of shots on greens with more than one level is indispensable.

The green with a high level in the center and low levels at the sides, gives splendid value to the straightly played shot; and the green with a low center, and with both sides made of higher levels, is even finer, for the direction of the shot may be changed, and the player required to direct his ball to either one of the high levels at the side. It will readily be seen that if it reaches the wrong side, he must putt downhill across the lower center, and again uphill to the higher level beyond.

On such a green very fine approach putting is demanded for any man to go down in two putts; and all these variations of the green make for more interest and better placement of shots.

The punch bowl green, and the saucer green, are especially valuable where the shot is blind, or semi-blind, and are greatly superior to complicated or even flat greens. The drainage of such greens requires special ingenuity, and this must be arranged carefully. Where it is more practical to drain the green at one side, an opening may be made there; and if a mound is placed high and short of the opening, very few balls which reach the green will roll off through it, because it may be rather narrow, and with a protecting, overlapping roll in front and another roll behind it. A slow-running ball, if there is not too much drop to the opening, will not run down it, while the fast-moving ball will go beyond it; and most balls will be stopped by the mound in front. Such a green is No. 3 at Ojai, which drains at the right hand side, and is of the punch bowl variety.

Protecting mounds which are staggered, may also be used at the back on greens which slope away from the line of play; and very few balls will roll through the opening left for the drainage, provided, of course, its fall is not too great.

The hog-back green with the high center may only be used when the side compartments are sufficiently large to make a dividing roll between two properly-

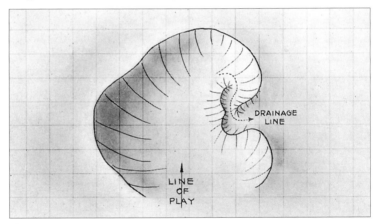

Surface drainage of a punch bowl green by means of rolls. Drainage at right. Drainage between rolls should be wide enough to play from.

TENTH GREEN, 330 YARDS, LA CUMBRE, SANTA BARBARA, CALIFORNIA.
A double level green, each side with its own approach.

VIEW FROM FIRST TEE; SHAUGHNESSY HEIGHTS CLUB, VANCOUVER, CANADA.

sized sections of the green. It must not slope too quickly and cause descending balls to shoot off the green. A ridge of this type is a wonderful hazard placed just short of a green, for most balls which do not reach the green will be deflected away from it. If there is such a hog back which is too narrow on its entire length to be made into a green, it is very easy to widen it on both sides and make the green of the necessary width to receive the shot as a saucer.

Traps on each side of the hog back will stop the balls from rolling down too great a hill; and at the sides of the green they will necessitate a pitch shot for those who go right or left.

Greens may be long and narrow, wide and shallow; in fact of every shape; but the great thing to be noted is that they must adhere to three most important principles: First, their utility for the shot required, which includes correct orientation or visibility; second, their utility as to all drainage and other physical needs; third, their beauty taken as an individual unit, and also as they appear in the landscape.

The man who can comply with these principles, and also diversify his greens, is a successful golf architect.

Greens with rolls at their sides have been criticised because if a ball played for the green descends on the inward side of a mound, it is turned to the green, and this is claimed to aid a poor shot. The defense to this charge is sound and practical. Make the green the proper size including rolls which will deflect inward. Shots which hit on the outside of the rolls will be sent

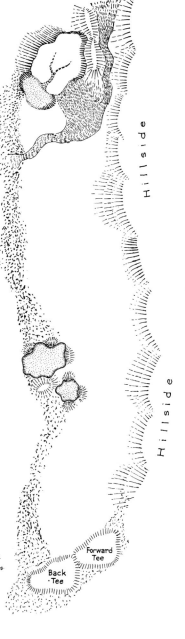

**FIRST, 368 YARDS,
BELVEDERE CLUB,
CHARLEVOIX, MICHIGAN.**

The green is situated at the base of a hill. An approach shot played too safely will find itself in the hollow to the right. There are two methods of approach— either a bold lofted shot right on the pin or a running stroke through the low hollow.

Drawing by William Watson, Golf Course Architect.

LEGEND

Tees.

Rough.

Sand Pits.

Rounded Mounds.

Large Grassy Hollows.

Shallow Grassy Swales in Greens.

Slopes.

Hillsides.

Trees.

Hillside

Hillside

Forward Tee

Back Tee

Photograph by Rau.   *(Ross.)*

PUNCH BOWL AT SEA VIEW, NEAR ATLANTIC CITY, N. J.
Additions by Wilson-Tillinghast and Robinson.

Photograph by Gabriel Moulin.   *Courtesy Olympic Club.*   *(Watson and Whiting.)*
GREEN OF NINTH HOLE, OCEAN LINKS, OLYMPIC CLUB, SAN FRANCISCO, CALIFORNIA.
Length, 528 yards. The drive comes over cliff in distance. A double level high at back.

away from the green possibly into a trap.   More is gained in visibility by the contrast of the rolls than is lost by balls aided by their slopes.

In greens which have narrow entrances for the running shot, or which have only one entrance for it, do not forget that a grade which helps the ball to reach the green increases the width of an opening, because a shot reaching it at an angle which would ordinarily take it away from the green—if there were no slope— will be guided toward the green by the slope.   This applies most forcibly to a ball arriving at proper speed.

In summing up, remember that your utility and your beauty may and must be combined.   If you fail in either your course is without true merit.

VI

ADAPTING THE COURSE TO THE GROUND

IN THE actual plan for the course, the greatest care must be taken to secure the full value, with the least congestion, moderate expense in construction and other necessary fundamentals.

The proper solution is much on the order of a chess problem; the first effort is not generally the best.

One must study the land and also the contour map before being able to commence work. Sometimes it

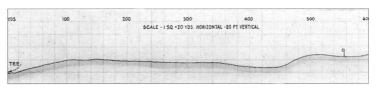

How the lay of the land at the Red Hill Country Club, California, was ideal for a fine three-shot hole; the first hill furnished a driving hazard, the second necessitated a pitch to the green.

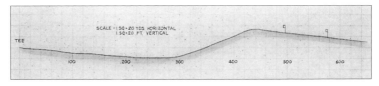

Such a contour as the above should, if possible, be used from right to left; otherwise the second is blind and the rise of the ground too great for a long shot.

seems as though the course worked itself out. One can readily see just where the holes will fit one after the other; but as a rule this is not the case, and the man who tries to walk over the ground once, and lay

Photograph by Graham.   A NEW GREEN ON THE FAMOUS EIGHTH AT PEBBLE BEACH, CALIFORNIA (400 YARDS).   *Courtesy Hotel Del Monte.*

The second shot goes across the chasm.

Hole originally designed by Hobart. New green constructed by Mackenzie and Hunter.

out the course as he goes, cannot expect to secure fine results. The starts and finishes should be worked out first, and very often the difficulty in securing a situation suitable for these will determine the clubhouse site. As one learns the land and its possibilities, one commences to visualize greens, tee shots, and even entire fairways, which appear here and there disjointedly, just as one discovers parts of a picture puzzle which stand out clearly, but do not fit with any other pieces already patched together. Such finds should be sketched on a map for future reference.

Among the green sites which stand out are some which are too fine to lose, and other holes must be discovered which will link them together. When you are able to so connect several holes with a start or finish, you are beginning to place the framework of your golf course.

Soon you have before you a part of a nine, and the puzzle is to bring this into touch with your finish and your start of the same nine. Here it is that the one-shot holes are so valuable, and one reason it was suggested earlier in this text that five of these be used, because one shotters aid you in welding the disconnected links of your golf chain.

Too often you must either give up one promising hole or another, as you will frequently find it impossible to bring these together; and to arrive correctly at your solution you should work out problems on your contour map and on paper, and decide which has the most superlative worth. Unless the solution comes

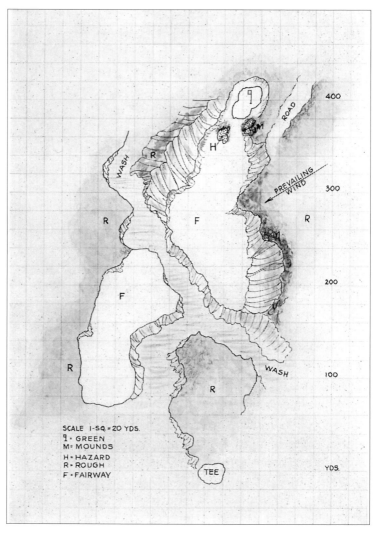

SKETCH OF NATURAL DOUBLE FAIRWAYS, EACH WITH AN OPTIONAL DRIVING
HAZARD.
There are many places where existing conditions make a beautiful natural hole.

with reasonable quickness on the ground, you will soon be marking up maps at a great rate, and a little trick taught me by Willie Tuckie, Jr., is a wonderful aid. Your map is, of course, contoured to scale, and you can cut out of blotting paper miniature fairways, making them also to the same scale as the map; it is easy to place them on your contour map with thumb tacks, first having your map on a board.

You will find that by hinging these little fairways at or about the 200-yard mark, you can make them follow the contours on the map as dog legs or straight holes. You can play with them just as if they were picture puzzle units; and by making them of different lengths, all to scale, with their width corresponding to that of fairways from 65 to 80 yards wide, the one shotters unhinged and the three-shot holes hinged twice, you will find them of the utmost help.

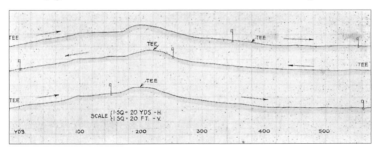

The upper line depicts the way a hill was treated years ago in Massachusetts. Both holes were poor and the first especially bad, as only the longest hitter could see the green on his second, and the top of the hill had rocky outcroppings which caused many balls to be lost.

The two lower lines show better ways of using these contours, both getting rid of objectionable blindness and avoiding playing over the rock-covered summit. The central line solution is the best, but lower plan an improvement over the uppermost if the play must be from left to right. Arrows indicate direction of play. By drawing such rough sectional contours one may easily work out the best way to place new holes.

Such a plan gives you clear thinking as you work on your map, and avoids the annoyance of constantly using new maps or erasing lines already drawn and found useless.

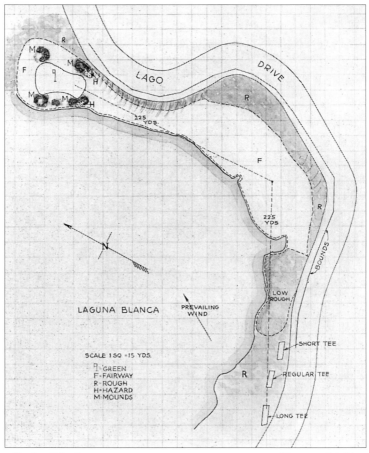

Courtesy Peter Bryce.   *(Thomas and Bell.)*

FOURTH, 426 YARDS, CENTER TEE, SANTA BARBARA, CALIFORNIA.

This hole was easily laid out from the tee site when first seen and the first three holes were arranged to end at its beginning.

The contour map is of the greatest assistance, but the ground must be checked with it, the locations carefully marked and oriented both on the ground and on the map with exactness and agreement.

Next, the visibility and playing value of the holes claim attention.

Stand on a selected tee site and work out various schemes of playing to the green. If, for example, you have a low ridge at the left of your proposed fairway, which slopes to the right, and will "kick" a ball landing on it from left to right, you at once have something to work with. One solution would be to make a trap which cannot be carried in the fairway to the right of the slope, so that if a golfer lands his tee shot on the low roll of the ridge to the left of the trap, it will bounce forward, gain additional run by the down slope to the right, and run around the trap. If, on the other hand, it is played straight on the line of the trap, it cannot carry it or run through it. This arrangement calls for a particular shot from the tee. Next you must work out the path for the man who has not enough length to play for this running shot around the hazard. He may play short, or possibly you can let him go to the right of the trap with open fairway and an opening to the green on his side; but because he has avoided the issue of the difficult running shot past the trap, he has a much longer second shot to the green, as the hole has become a dog leg for him.

In this proposition it would seem that you should construct a hazard short of the green on its left or the

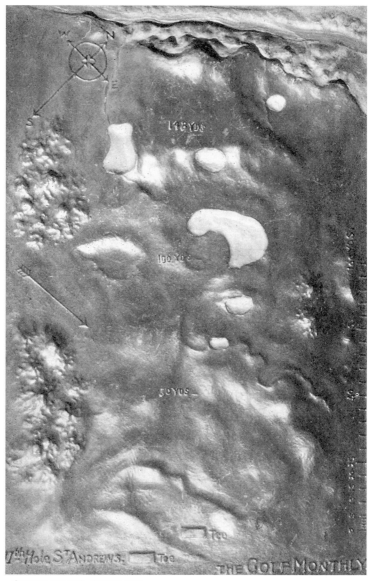

Courtesy Fox Hills Country Club.

From a photograph of model of Eleventh, St. Andrews, Scotland—a hole which has been reproduced on several courses in America. Such adaptations are only advisable where the topography is almost identical. The famous old hole will be reproduced at the Fox Hills Country Club, Los Angeles.

long man's side, thereby compelling him to pitch to the green, because he is closer. With this plan you have a lot of strategy for the hole; but before thinking of going ahead with this arrangement, you must check the feasibility of your tactics on the ground itself. To do this try shots from your tee and see where they hit; play them both for the short man and for the long man; persevere until you know the actual playing value. If you cannot hit them properly yourself, get some one who can. In this test do not overlook the problem of the wind.

It is not hard to estimate the run of the ball from where it lands, and you must judge of this not from your conditions on the raw ground, but by what they will be on the fairway later, taking into consideration the speed to be developed on that type of fairway. A fore-caddie, or some one placed near the landing of the shots, will give the carry very exactly.

Then the most important thing—the one of superlative need—is to go to the spots on the fairway where both the short and the long drives reach, and see what visibility you have from such locations for the approach.

That is where so many golf holes go wrong; they may have the right length and the proper carrying hazards, as far as the distances of the shot are concerned, but one cannot see the green and it is not oriented.

After you have experimented with drives on a two shotter, and stood on the points selected as placements, you will be able to decide whether your first plan for the hole is likely to succeed. By hitting more shots from the positions reached by the drives, you may determine the type of shot you can best require for that green, and consider how the green will contrast with the shot of the preceding and the following holes, and also with other shots on the course.

You will be able to judge of the size which your green should be in order properly to receive particular shots, and whether your contours, as they exist, will aid in this reception, and if not, what you must do to change them so that they will not penalize a correctly played effort. If the pitch shot is not right for the

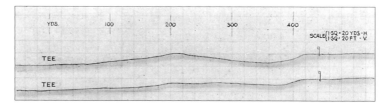

Two sections of a good way to use a hill. The player must hit a fine ball from the tee in order to see the green when playing his second. Such a hole should have two tees, one nearer the hill summit for the short player. The lower hill line is better than the upper for the reason that a long drive does not have a downhill lie. This plan ought not to be used more than once on a course unless unavoidable. There should be no artificial carry from the tee as the hill supplies strategy by its blindness. The green must have a wide opening to give the man playing a blind shot a chance, but should be fairly small to require accuracy.

long man on account of the contours, it will be better to change the stroke to a running one, perhaps giving him an opening from his side. Where it can be done, it is more advisable to use the ground that you have, and make the play fit the ground, rather than to force the ground to conform to the shot. This should only be done where you have too many of the same kind

EIGHTH GREEN, PALM BEACH, FLORIDA.
The rolls on this green fade imperceptibly into contacting contours.

WHITLOCK GOLF CLUB, NEAR MONTREAL, CANADA.

on other holes, under which situation you must consider which hole will be more easily altered, and give the most value for change. If your first plan is not perfect, you must work out others until you are sure you have provided for all contingencies.

Slopes, hills, mounds, or any other natural contour, which affect the roll or run of a ball, are aids on all parts of your fairways; and your strategy should, if possible, hinge on them. If you have no natural contours, you may build them.

Compel your golfers to try for certain shots by these natural or artificial hazards, and teach them to play different types of strokes, and, best of all, to place them.

One properly made blind, or semi-blind green is permissible. Two such shots will not be objectionable provided you orient them carefully so that the golfer can learn to play for the green by something near it which you place for him to see and judge by. Too many of these holes are to be avoided.

Construction which makes it possible to visualize a green is very important. A green may be actually visible, but because there is nothing to throw it out, it is blinder than a truly blind hole which has been properly oriented by mounds placed in front or near it, from which one may deduce its location.

Furthermore, if such a blind green is on the punch-bowl type, it is more satisfactory. One hole of this kind which always comes to my mind as almost perfect, was old No. 5 at Huntingdon Valley in Pennsylvania, and this was a one-shot hole. Other original holes on that order were a two-shot hole at the Seaview Golf Club, near Atlantic City, New Jersey, which was well oriented at the sides of the blind green, and another very interesting saucer-shaped green at Woods Hole, Massachusetts.

Where it is difficult to provide for drainage, it is not feasible to use a punch bowl. For a blind shot, where the punch bowl is thereby impractical, it is best to make a green nearly twice as large as would ordinarily be used for that particular distance, an illustration of which is the very large green at No. 17 at Ojai Valley in California. By the large green you accomplish almost the same purpose as with a punch bowl, which is to have your ball stay on the green and not require too exact a placement.

The blame given a blind hole is not fair under many conditions. No one ever thinks that in order to secure a very fine No. 8 it is necessary to have a blind No. 3, for in no other way can the architect link together his sequence of nine holes, or his loop of six, or whatever his problem may be.

The blind shot from the tee to the fairway must also be oriented, and such a variation is valuable to break a long climb. An example of this arrangement is to be found on No. 8 at the La Cumbre course near Santa Barbara. Here No. 7 green is part way up a steep grade, after which the golfer walks higher to No. 8 tee, and on arrival there drives over the balance of the hill. This practice splits a hill into three walks

Photograph by Martin. (*Thomas and Bell.*)
SEVENTEENTH, 130 YARDS, OJAI, CALIFORNIA.
A blind one-shot hole oriented by tree at left and bank beyond. The green is made large to hold the shot.

Photograph by Hayward. (*Strong.*)
NINTH GREEN, MANOIR RICHELIEU COURSE, MURRAY BAY, P. Q., CANADA.
Courtesy of "Canadian Golfer."

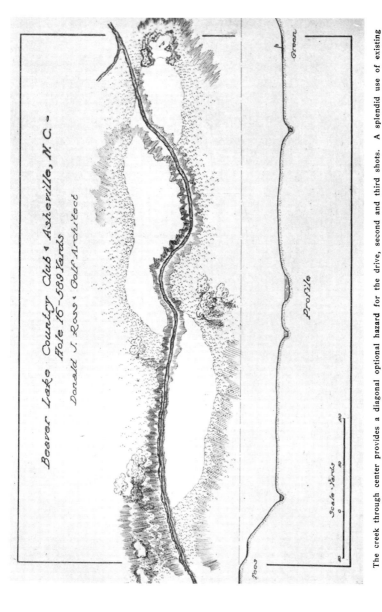

Beaver Lake Country Club ◦ Asheville, N.C. ◦
Hole 16 – 589 Yards

Donald J. Ross ◦ Golf Architect

Green

Profile

Scale Yards

0   40   80

The creek through center provides a diagonal optional hazard for the drive, second and third shots. A splendid use of existing conditions. A superb three-shot hole.

with two rests. No. 7 green provided a rest while the others were putting; the second rest came on No. 8 tee where each man had a rest while the others drove. These rests are most acceptable. On the Santa Barbara hole noted, the length of No. 8 is increased by having the tee below the hill, and is the only place on that course where there is a blind tee shot, and therefore satisfactory as a variation.

One frequently hears, or reads, that it is very important not to add length to a hole, and thereby spoil it; but often it is of as much moment to increase the distance, and, in consequence, produce a finer one. In this connection it is very much easier to make a superlative long two-shot hole than it is to make the unique short two shotter; so it is only where the contours are most indicative, with a certain green and tee placement, that a short two shotter will be ruined by increased yardage.

In laying out a course, there are some who, when possible, make two circles of the sequence of play—nine holes in each circle. The inner circle will include all territory within its rim, and the outer circle will contain everything beyond the inner one with the boundary on the order of a circumference.

There are others who go out one side of a square tract and back the other from a central point; and it is generally customary to use the boundary on the slicing side.

There are many practical schemes for fairly flat ground, but where the country is broken with heavy

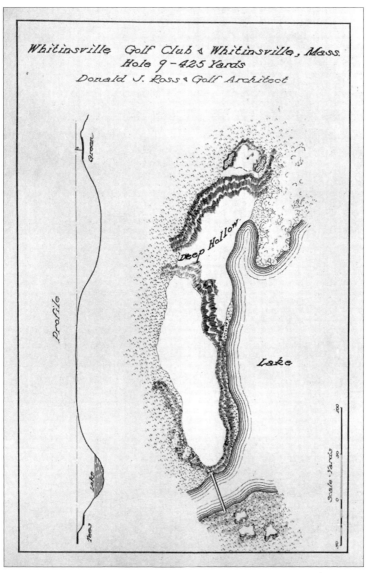

Whitinsville Golf Club ~ Whitinsville, Mass.
Hole 9 - 425 Yards
Donald J. Ross ~ Golf Architect

A fine type of drive and full iron or spoon to the green. The high plateau is a
most suitable landing place for drive and gives unobstructed view of green.

contours, and very imperative hazards, the course must be placed to suit the land; and it is out of the question to consider any particular formal plan. On broken territory it is harder to find the best solutions, yet such a location gives diversity already built. To lay out a course over rough terrain, and to economize space without losing value, requires the greatest patience.

After you have your sequence in hypothesis, it is mandatory to check it accurately on the property. The greens, the fairways and the tees should be staked, and the work must be oriented by an engineer. When the ground is carefully plotted, and no fairway, green or tee interferes with any other, or is interfered with by any other, then, and then only, may one begin to feel assurance that a correct solution has been attained.

In so checking your course, you will often find situations which may appear dangerous from a congestion standpoint, but which, in actual play, will not be of any real menace, for appearances indicating interference are sometimes deceptive. As a case in point, there is a nest of two tees and two greens on the South course of the Los Angeles Country Club, and their situation looks congested, but under playing test has never caused trouble.

On the other hand, there are many groupings which do not seem likely to cause interference, but which, after play, are found to be most unsatisfactory; so that it is of the greatest importance to study adjacent units carefully and avoid difficulty of this kind.

Greens must not be so placed that shots from tees or other fairways reach them, but fairways, especially

Courtesy of Donald Ross. (*Ross.*)

FOURTEENTH, AT DUNEDIN ISLES, FLORIDA.

This is a dog leg as indicated by dotted line; the pond is artificial and the green of the plateau type. An illustration of a made hole on uninteresting flat ground.

if adjacent to others, must be expected to receive a certain number of shots from tees or fairways of other holes.

Some writers recommend that tees be placed forward from the last green—never sideways or partly backward; but this is not always feasible. Yet, this practice is advisable where possible; and there is no excuse for a walk which takes one back toward the shot to the green one is leaving, especially if the walk is blind. Still there is such a walk on a well-known course.

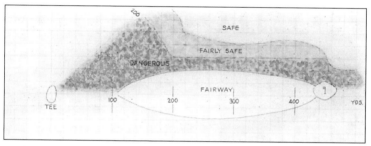

Any unprotected spot within 200 yards of a fairway runs a risk of being hit; but experience has shown that many positions are immune, or nearly so.

Shots from the tee are more dangerous than any others because they are longer, and more are hit from one location.

Without considering wind or natural protection the chart above shows the dangerous positions to the left from the tee and fairway as outlined, and it will be realized that the nearer to tee or fairway the greater is the danger.

All these questions are matters of balance, and may be successfully worked out on a tract with sufficient adaptable acreage.

In the matter of congestion, the handling of a gallery is very difficult on adjacent fairways, and even in small tournaments such galleries greatly interfere with players behind a feature match, and are unfair to those contestants. This is another argument in favor of separate fairways; and certainly, near your finishing holes there should be ample room provided for galleries on any courses which expect to hold important tournaments.

In all these equations various individual situations alter cases; and artificial hazards will protect walks and greens if there are no natural ones. Paths should be safe, and by requiring the walker to go somewhat out of his way, danger is avoided; otherwise the golfer will always go in the straightest line possible to his next tee.

There are examples where a walk from a green goes straight in front of another tee, and the user of the walk is unseen as he comes up a hill; this danger is without excuse.

Where broken country and flat country are adjacent, it will be found very easy and practical, in order to economize land and avoid too much grading, to place your tees a short distance in the broken land, and let the player drive over some rough terrain to a flat landing place beyond. In the same way it is advisable and interesting to build your greens for short second shots, or for short one-shot holes, a certain distance into the rough country, which will provide natural hazards for the green. Under few situations will it be found practicable to play a long second shot into rough country which continues for the distance re-

Courtesy of "Canadian Golfer."

FOURTH GREEN, ALOGONQUIN, ST. ANDREWS, N. B.
A Canadian Pacific Railway Course.

Photograph by Martin.   *(Thomas and Bell.)*

FIFTEENTH, 380 YARDS, OJAI, CALIFORNIA.
View from tee—forced carry 100 yards.
This hole demands a hooked drive as the fairway to green runs to the left after the carry. An example
of placing a tee' in broken ground and driving to a flat landing place beyond.

quired of such a shot, because there must be a safe way provided for the short man.

Do not judge of your distances by pacing; check them by shots and by accurate measurements with instruments. You will find by this method how short a distance some shots will carry, which you would otherwise think were of greater length. You will also find that a slight rise in the fairway, or an adverse wind, or sandy ground, greatly affect the distance of a shot. The playing value of Pine Valley is much longer than its actual yardage.

You must remember that atmospheric conditions affect the ball's flight. If there is cold the ball is not so resilient and does not travel well. If the air is heavy with humidity, this shortens its length, while in a very dry atmosphere, under warm conditions, the ball will fly further.

These factors should be considered, and are additional arguments for the placement of extra tees.

Rain, which makes the fairway slow, is another consideration in the playing length of golf holes, but winds are the most changing of all climatic conditions. In a country where there is a prevailing wind, the value of holes is more constant. Under dry ground conditions the run of the ball is largely increased, and all these things must be studied; their acknowledgment is the reason for the general omission, except on short shots, of carrying hazards which extend completely across the fairway, and give no option.

Not only may extra tees be arranged in the same line of play, and at different distances, but tees moved to one side or the other greatly affect the strategy of any hole, especially where there are prevailing cross winds.

A very interesting way of checking length is to note your distances by sequence of yardage, as well as by sequence of play. If you compare this sequence with that given in the chapter on "Different Courses," and consider the actual playing value of the land, you will have a good idea of your true yardage.

Your traps must be adapted to the ground as well as your greens and tees. It has been an old saying, and quoted in a number of books, that "no hazard which is visible is unfair"—or words to that effect—and most certainly every carrying hazard should be visible except under some special condition. Therefore, place your hazards on slight rises, if possible, which makes them more natural, without additional work; and if high spots are not in the right locations you must build your hazards above the surrounding ground, so that they may be seen and oriented. It is always advisable to show at least some little patch of sand above the surrounding ground level in order that the golfer may observe it from most positions; and it is remarkable how a little gleam of sand throws out its environment by virtue of contrast.

Notwithstanding the old saying regarding the fairness of visible hazards, the writer believes that many hazards are unfair because they are unnecessary, and not contained in the stategy of the hole. To penalize without method is certainly improper; and carries which give no alternative line but the wearisome

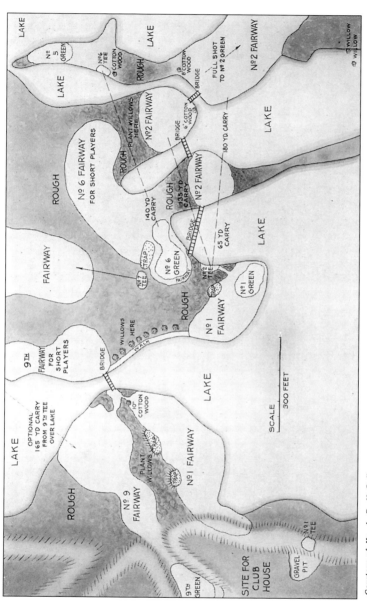

Courtesy of Mr. A. B. McGaffey.

DESIGNED FROM CONTOUR MAP FOR COURSE AT ALBUQUERQUE, N. M.

Note how holes are adapted to existing hazards.

(*Thomas.*)

process of playing short, border on injustice, and rightfully cause criticism.

On rocky ground be sure that you have sufficient depth of soil, or arrange for additional depth, so that your cup may be cut on any part of the green.

Before finally passing on your entire layout as satisfactory, you must consider very carefully the pars of your holes. It is unfortunate, after a course is completed, to find that the playing value is not as the pars were expected to work out. Sometimes you will discover that one of your long holes plays a fairly easy par 4 instead of the par 5 which you anticipated; and it is on the short three-shot holes, or long two-shot holes, that the greatest accuracy must be used in checking the distances, and the conditions which affect the ground speed. Before determining your length and par, the latter must work out logically before the

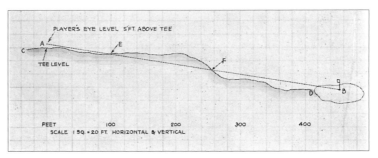

Straight line, A B, shows line of vision of player. Irregular line, C D, shows cross section of ground. Circle with flag denotes green and pin.

In making hole visible do not take off ground in flat slab as indicated by line, A B. Commencing at E dish the cut, widening it gradually to F. At E, such swale should be width of tee, at F, nearly width of green. Such practice is more economical in construction and more natural.

Illustration of No. 9, Whitemarsh, Pennsylvania, which the writer helped to construct, in 1908, was improved later by dish method, noted in illustration.

The same method may be used going uphill, and is also useful in openings to greens between traps when green is above stance of shot.

course is constructed, because afterwards a course is quickly judged by the playing value of its pars, most particularly from the back tees.

Adaptation of your course to your ground will also be a vital element in the matter of expense in your construction, as well as all the other equations which concern its playing value, and the comfort of your membership. It would seem wise to consult with those who have built courses in your nearest neighborhood, and secure from them advice as to various matters which have caused them trouble in construction and operation, and try beforehand to prepare for such, and to eliminate them where possible.

VII

THE ABILITY TO CREATE

AS IMPORTANT as the ability to plan the general layout and to build it so that it combines beauty and utility, is the gift of visualizing before the work is begun what may be effected.

In the old days when one started to build a green, one just "went at it" and built it, and mistakes which developed by this haphazard method were ever new and surprising, although the size of the green and the kind of shot which was needed to reach it were known beforehand. Nevertheless, the entire scheme of the hole was vague and not a complete proposition worked out by scale drawings from tee to green, but the old method was supported by the incorrect theory that it was best to trap the fairway and the green later on. So the greens were built in those times by rule of thumb, with farm hands to move the soil; and many of them had never seen a golf shot played. Yet, even among these raw tillers we found every so often, just as we do today, a man who was an artist.

During the past few years I have had three men of this type turn up. One was an old Irishman in the crew at the Los Angeles Municipal course, another a young cowboy from Arizona, and lately a ranchman from Utah built me some lovely bunkers. More often it is necessary to toil with your labor, many of whom

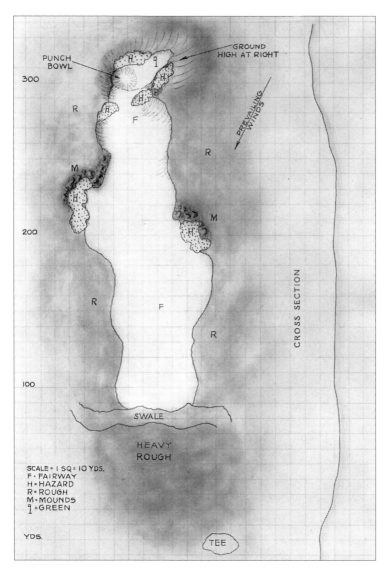

Sketch from description by George Duncan of a short two shotter which he considers the finest of this type. The punch bowl is part of the green. If the flag is at the right on the high level above the punch bowl, a placed drive near the left-hand fairway trap opens the pin to the shot. If the cup is in the bowl a shot from tee should be in the center to give a running approach between the guarding traps.

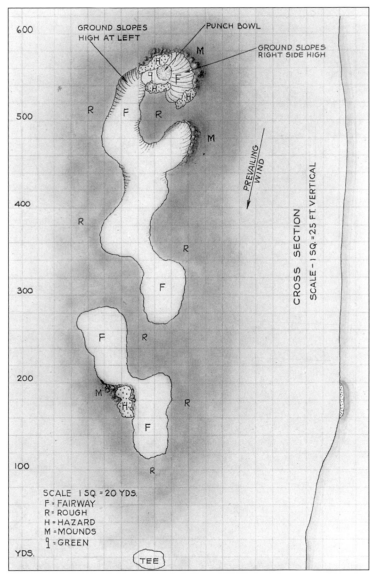

An adaptation of the green described by Duncan. The ground near green is nearly flat and as this is a three shotter, changes are necessary in the strategy; but the novelty of a green containing punch bowl and high level is secured. To reproduce a hole under any but similar conditions is usually inadvisable.

have been taught to construct lawns and the like in straight lines, and who insist on making everything smooth and straight rather than in the curves desired.

The first accurate plans I saw were those of Donald Ross, when I worked on a green committee where he laid out the course. This did me a lot of good, for up to that time, as noted, the work had been without definite scheme.

Next I saw some plasticine models, and they were most interesting to me. I started work at once with moulding clay, and my next course was built by an engineer who reproduced my models by cross section. This course was a success, and its greens satisfied me more than the ones I had formerly built; the value of models was very evident. Nevertheless, models must be used with the greatest care, for there are bad faults which crop up when you work with them. They must fit in their places with the utmost accuracy; levels must be taken with exactness, and the scale of the model be quite correct both horizontally and vertically. Even then, if you have not visualized it properly, and explained it clearly, it is likely to turn into a terrible object if you go away and let some one, who has not the three necessary qualifications of being an artist, and an engineer, and understanding golf strategy, try to reproduce it.

One of the most serious matters in working with a model is to place it correctly; not only must the green entrance face as desired, but the exact level of the flat base should be very carefully arranged. The slightest tilt in any direction will greatly affect the finished work. The proper placement of the model must be considered in connection with visibility and other practical necessities.

Nevertheless, where one cannot be on the ground during construction, a model accurately worked out, carefully checked and rightly placed by a man who knows the underlying principles of golf is very satisfactory.

The very opposite to this theory is that of one who works his ground before his eyes, moulding it during its growth as he wishes it, and by this method producing the result with a minimum of effort. Such a man does not proceed primarily by means of a contour map as does the architect for houses and grounds. He commences to visualize as he moulds his creation. Any one who can do this, and do it well, has a great gift. His plan is an improvement over the original method of going at a green and "just making it," because he has ideals for which he is working, and he moulds his green much as the other man moulds the plasticine model, whereas in the old days when we started a green we had only hazy ideas of what we desired to produce. The whole theory of the fairway and strategy of that hole was not complete, and therefore our greens did not fit into the general scheme.

As for my own method, I find guessing levels very deceptive. I need a contour map* and a few levels on the ground. My scale sketch of the plan of the hole works out for me the length of the shot from the

---

*Where exact cost is desired contractors can give estimates from contour maps of earth to be moved.

Photograph by Black D. (Behr.)

ELEVENTH, LAKESIDE GOLF CLUB, HOLLYWOOD, CALIFORNIA.

A double fairway hole divided by sand—combining clever strategy, splendid orientation of fairways and artistic beauty of outline.

tee, and the length and character of the shot to the green; and by my tests of carry with clubs and balls I know where the golf shots will go on the fairway later on. I work out my strategy for the entire hole. I visualize my green beforehand; I check such visualizations by levels. If I have an engineer in charge of the work who does not understand golf, I give him a model to work with in addition to the sketch of the hole; and I check his stakes after he has the green cross sectioned and oriented on the ground. If I have a man in charge in whom I have absolute confidence, I need only give him a sketch to scale as a plan of the hole, and a sketch as to elevation. Then, as the green develops, I can see things to improve in it. I must always pass on it before it is sown to seed.

As further considerations, the green must not only be composed of proper material, so that it will not become packed with a hard surface below grass, which causes the shots to rebound from it, but it must have been built in its raised portions so that it will not change its final levels, for should it sink on a high side the result is disastrous.

Lately we have ascertained green drainage by the flowing of water on it and noting the result.

Fortunately, the building of a green has considerable latitude. In some respects it is not a thing of minute exactness as to measurements. The slopes may vary. Even the levels may differ a few inches in height from the proposed plan without danger to the playing value, but woe be to one who does not understand and visualize the theory of the play of any given hole. He must provide each golfer with a reasonable route of safety, and the green must properly receive shots played from the points on the fairway indicated by the strategy.

The drainage must be perfect; the putting surface faultless; the direct or indirect visibility supplied must be without flaw; and the green must have individuality. It is necessary for a problem to exist from tee to green —a problem to be solved differently by various players, and such green must be built by a man who has the ability to create. He must know in advance what he desires to produce, and must then produce it.

There are many places where it is essential to grade a hole to secure distance, variety, or visibility, and again, grading will improve a hole to a great extent, under other conditions; but natural contours should be changed only where necessary, and many existing ones may be emphasized for superlative value.

The new No. 1 at La Cumbre, Santa Barbara, is a good example of the necessity of changing grades. Here there was only one possible route from the club-house to Potter Lake, and the chance to play around that body of water and secure its strategy of water hazards. The tee of No. 1 was already placed in a fine, natural location, but in the direct line of play a big, natural roll blocked further progress to the hole at about 365 yards from the tee; and if the green were placed short of this roll, a long walk to the next tee was unavoidable.

Photograph by Prentiss.

ON A LONG TWO SHOTTER, SEVENTEENTH GREEN, LAKE OSWEGO, PORTLAND, OREGON.

Note how the dark trees orient the green and its bold outlines.

Courtesy of H. Chandler Egan.

(*Egan.*)

It was, therefore, very easy to cut a pathway for the finish of the hole and of the green through one side of the obstructing mound, obtaining the additional distance, and cutting out the long walk.

There are situations where it is unwise and difficult to change the natural contours; or where poorly modelled additions detract from the natural beauty already existing. The chief of this latter type is where a slope falls away from the line of play, for often this slope is built up at the back, and after being so built is not allowed to float gradually into the contour behind, but goes down with too upright a line. If there is a rim placed at the back of such a green, this rim adds to the ungainliness at the back. Very often it is feasible on such a slope to make a green with a double level, or at least have a fairway dip before the green itself is made. This decreases the amount of earth required in the fill, and makes a much more pleasing contour; but such a green should be made for a running shot.

Frequently, it is found beneficial to fill up a dry wash, or a small creek, for use of fairway or green, and in this situation a proper-sized pipe will carry off water which formerly ran through.

The scale on which one makes rolls and mounds depends on the scale of the existing contours, otherwise your creations will not balance with the landscape. Thus, on a flat plain the rolls must be of larger base to the height than would be required in a narrow valley; and no matter the size of the green itself, this necessity of proportion holds true.

Where there is sandy and gravelly ground, one may place traps or hollows below the ground level. These are advisable around a green if raised traps would spoil the visibility by coming between the line of vision of the player and the green; but any contours, unless there is a way to drain them, are abominations on clay courses.

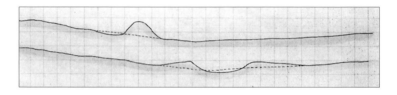

The upper lines show a fairway with the hazard incorrectly placed, being too high and insufficient in width for the long, easy-flowing lines around it, and in danger of filling with water from its upper side.

Below is the same fairway line with a hazard which by its width and height fits into its place in proper proportion, and in addition is protected from surface drainage.

Furthermore, the lower hazard will stop more running shots but give the man trapped a reasonable chance for recovery.

When the ground is rocky, the entire hazard may readily be built above the existing level.

Fairway hazards should give a man a chance for a long recovery, but they must be sufficiently wide to stop a hard-hit ball. It would seem that 30 feet was the minimum of their width, but the side of the hazard should be above that of the adjacent fairway ahead, requiring the player to loft the ball quickly in order to secure distance. Hazards close to the green may often ask for the explosion shot; they may be deep and not unnecessarily wide, especially where they are called upon to penalize a pitch shot which is short.

Photograph by Rau.

(Crump and Colt.)

TENTH, 134 YARDS, PINE VALLEY, N. J.

A beautiful pitch—well oriented by natural sand. A superlative creation.

Cross-fire holes, where one fairway plays across another, are out of the question, although this situation exists at old St. Andrews.

Generally speaking, adjacent fairways should be divided by rough and traps and the planting of trees; but on small tracks, where the holes must be close together, this is ofttimes impossible, and is a very strong additional objection to fairways which are close together.

Under such propinquity the dangers to tees or to greens from either tee or fairway shots are the most serious menaces.

When playing parallel holes in a narrow valley, it is very easy to throw the play away from the center by the proper placing of traps, and also making the green entrances from the sides; in fact, such practice is, of course, valuable in other situations.

When playing adjacent parallel fairways, it is also a help to have the lines of play in the same direction, as this lessens danger.

Careful juggling of tees and greens will cause a minimum of peril and congestion, but under these changes the full value of shots will not be obtained.

A piece of land on which you can place 18 holes without interference with one another, may be made the most of, and assume ideal character. While there may be room to crowd 36 holes into the same space, yet, when fairways are adjacent, value must be sacrificed to safety, and it is impossible to secure as many superlative features.

Traps in proper positions force players away from congestion. Trees may be planted to give safety; mounds will often aid the situation; but in placing trees and mounds beware of making a blind condition. High, closely woven wire fences to give protection to a tee, or to guard a green from a tee shot, are only used as a last resort. They are very unsightly, but where real danger exists they are advisable; and when used, should be covered by vines. Generally, these situations may be avoided, but there are occasions when lack of space makes them necessary.

In the building of hazards, there is as much need of foreseeing what will happen when the ball is trapped and the golfer forced to extricate it, as there is in visualizing any other part of golf construction.

In sandy or even somewhat sandy country, the play out of a hazard takes care of itself almost entirely; but in a land of clay, where sand is placed on top of it in hazards, the contours must be made so that the sand is in sufficient quantity always to be deep enough to keep the descending blade from contact with the hard ground below. For this reason gentle slopes which hold the sand are better than severe slopes from which it will be displaced; and a straight bank in front of the player is better than an easier grade on which the ball will be in shallow, ever-moving sand.

Dr. Mackenzie, the noted Scotch architect, recently suggested that under such conditions a heavy clay might have the sand placed lightly on its surface and tamped into it, thus presenting the exterior appearance

Courtesy of Frank Meline Company.

VIEW FROM ELEVENTH TEE, BEL-AIR, CALIFORNIA.

(Thomas and Bell.)

A double-fairway hole—the path for the short player at right; the long man must carry knoll to left (center of picture and 160 yards from tee). Tee on side hill to give room for two holes in narrow canyon.

Photograph by Meeson.   *(Emmet.)*

SEVENTEENTH GREEN, ST. GEORGE'S GOLF AND COUNTRY CLUB, STONY BROOK, L. I.

This green is naturally placed and attractive.

Courtesy of Devereux Emmet.

Photograph by Chisholm.   *(Tucker and Son.)*

GREEN, TACOMA CLUB, WASHINGTON.

H. Chandler Egan and Forrest Watson in final of Pacific Northwest Championship, 1925.

of sand, but producing a surface down which the ball would roll to the deeper sand below. This should be valuable in the placing of sand for orientation; it would reduce upkeep, and apparently be satisfactory except at the point where the tamped sand ended and the deeper sand began—a small equation of the whole.

The course which has many lost balls is never popular, because it is a source of constant irritation, and this important feature must be carefully thought of beforehand.

The ability to create is to consider all the problems of a golf course. The architect must visualize the effect his work will produce from all angles of the game, as noted in the chapter on "Utility and Beauty."

VIII

THE BALANCE OF AREA

WHILE it is difficult to give any hard and fast rules as to the exact sizes in area of various parts of the golf course, nevertheless, figures may be supplied as to approximates required, if one takes varying factors into consideration.

Placing the different parts of the course in logical order, one would first study the size of tees, and this is, undoubtedly, the easiest of the propositions.

On Municipal courses with heavy congestion, and an average of many players every day, mat tees are the best solution.

For Club courses, with large playing memberships, and an average of from one hundred to one hundred and fifty a day, tee surfaces for holes on which wood is used from the tee should be not less than 2,000 square feet at a minimum; 2,500 would be a better area, and 3,000 square feet ample provision. On such courses for tees needing iron shots, a larger area is required; 2,500 square feet should be a minimum of surface. If several tees are used, put five-eighths of your area for the central tee; one-quarter for the back or championship tee, and one-eighth for the short tee location.

For smaller courses, where the average play would not exceed fifty a day, it would be advisable to use not less than half the maximum space figured for the larger

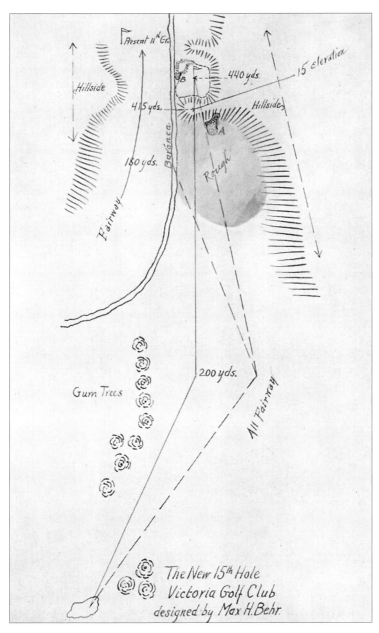

The New 15th Hole
Victoria Golf Club
designed by Max H. Behr

Riverside, California. To gain length trees must be risked, but Bunker B is the key to the second and in avoiding it Bunker A catches a weak shot. Placement required by long or short golfer. A novel and interesting arrangement with well-balanced areas.

courses, because, as a rule, clubs with a small playing membership desire the ultimate of perfection in up-keep.

For all tee surfaces it would be better if a consider-able extent of fairway were contoured and seeded; this could be cut as required, and a very large area thereby supplied, which would provide change tees; but some locations do not lend themselves to this practice.

The care of tees very greatly affects the situation. They should not be kept too damp, because this makes them cut more easily. The placing of markers, their thoughtful change, and, in addition, quick repairing of scarred portions, are important considerations.

In the matter of fairways the amount of traffic must be taken into account, because narrow fairways cause congestion; but, as a general rule, fairways should average from sixty-five to eighty yards in width for the reception of long tee shots.

Although it is very often advisable to provide fair-way immediately in front of tees, the first hundred yards should not be cut short as is the main body of the fairway. Frequently, there will be rough ground in front of the tee which should not be touched, but the short player should not have much over one hundred yards of ordinary rough to negotiate. At one hundred yards from the tee, a width of forty yards for the fair-way is ample. The width of the fairway should then increase up to one hundred and eighty yards from the tee, where it should have its greatest width. It should remain at this width to two hundred and fifty yards,

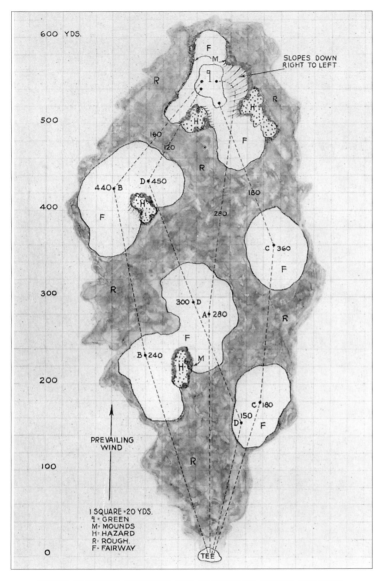

ISLAND FAIRWAYS DESIGNED FOR PLAYERS OF VARIED ABILITIES.
The objection to such holes is the great amount of land required and the extreme difficulty of securing a balance which demands that each class of players holds one line. (From original drawing.)

after which, on a two shotter, it may gradually decrease to the green; it should not exceed the green entrance unless on holes requiring exceptionally long shots to the green.

On three-shot holes the fairway should be kept at good width after reaching one hundred and eighty yards, until within short range of the green, where it should be narrow, except that on the few very long three shotters, where a long third is required to the green for perfect play, there should be fairways at the sides and back of the green. As in other matters, the location of your fairway near the green depends on the kind of shots which will be played to that green.

On many courses there are found unnecessarily wide fairways which increase the cost of upkeep.

On dog-leg holes the fairway should be wider at the angle of the dog leg, and, as with greens, the width of fairways should be governed by the shots they are designed to accommodate.

Island fairways provide strategy where the ball must be played over rough to secure an advantageous position before a chance at the green is obtainable. The island fairway has many attractive variations, but is not adaptable in a clay country with a long, dry season and artificial irrigation, where the rough has speed without vegetation. The fourth hole at Lido, Long Island, is a splendid example of island fairway with safe route for the average player.

The cutting of the sides of fairways should not be made in straight lines, for, as noted by numerous writers, the curves made by the edges of fairways

Courtesy of Canadian Golfer.

TORONTO GOLF CLUB, LONG BRANCH, ONTARIO, CANADA.

(*Colt.*)

enable players and caddies to mark more easily balls which go in the rough. Lately, on a number of courses where rough has no outstanding features, painted stakes have been placed so that balls may be more readily marked.

In the cutting of rough, great judgment must be used to cut it properly around traps, for where it is found that balls travel through certain traps, and run into the fairway beyond, rough may be left in front of the trap and also past it, but must not be kept too long, or lost balls will result. In this connection it is much better to have a ball stop in rough short of the trap, and secure a less penalty than if it had run over fairway into the trap, than it is for a ball to run through the trap into either rough or fairway beyond.

The size of traps should vary considerably; often a very small pot bunker on slightly raised ground is very valuable for orientation as well as for strategy, and small outcroppings of sand on natural or artificial mounds, near a green, are of much merit for the same reasons.

To stop a full drive, hazards will need more width as they are nearer the tee; certainly thirty feet of sand is the minimum, even when the hazard has some height. Sunken traps short of a green, and traps for orientation, especially with banks beyond them which are higher, may be made much smaller, particularly if the bank is fairly perpendicular.

Traps beyond greens to catch pitch shots which run over, need much less size than driving hazards, and usually less width than other green traps. The width and length of your hazards, the same as the width of your fairways and the location of your rough, should be made for the shot which is to be played on the hole, as well as for proper visibility. In addition, the finished production must conform with the adjacent ground for purposes of naturalness and beauty.

Where traps encroach on landing places on fair ways, such landing places should be much larger than greens made to receive the same shot, the dimensions of which are hereinafter explained. This applies to landing places whether they are surrounded by artificial hazards or rough.

Where a placement is demanded for purposes of strategy, the landing place for a drive at one hundred and sixty-five to two hundred and fifty yards, under average conditions, should have a width of from one hundred feet at the first distance, to one hundred and

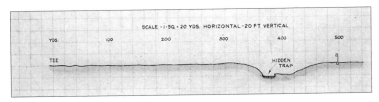

The clever principle of hidden trap used by Max Behr. The trap is fair because a good second goes beyond it, and after once playing the hole the golfer can visualize the position of trap by hill short of it.

fifty feet at the latter; but note that slopes affect such computations, because rolls which run toward the center of the fairway protect wild shots and nurse them to the fairway. Therefore, where these grades obtain,

Photograph by Gabriel Moulin.   *(Watson and Whiting.)*
TENTH HOLE, 185 YARDS, OCEAN LINKS, OLYMPIC COURSE, SAN FRANCISCO, CALIFORNIA.
A famous hole with proper green surface for reception of shot.
Courtesy of Olympic Club.

Photograph by Rau.   *(Crump and Colt.)*
THE FORCED CARRYING HAZARD FOR SECOND SHOT ON THE SEVENTH, PINE VALLEY, N. J.
(551 YARDS.)
An extremely large artificial hazard.

the landing place may be smaller. In addition to this, wind and the speed of the ground affect the proper size of landing points.

Fairway openings between hazards for long shots ought to be greater in width than openings for greens requiring the same shots; and fairway openings for short shots should be slightly wider than openings to greens for the same type of strokes.

It is impossible to give any absolutely hard and fast rules for these areas. The traps, the rough, the fairways and natural hazards must all be considered with the length of shots, and all are part of the strategy of each hole. Where these are balanced carefully, the hole is a pleasure to play upon; but where, for any reason, the balance is poor, the play of the hole will be seriously affected. Nevertheless, it is not difficult to work out landing places with the fairways and traps, and one should always give the benefit of the doubt to the player. Where there is a question, it is always more advisable to give the player more room in his landing places than it is to constrict them and err on the side of making a shot too difficult. If you cannot secure sufficient room, you must shorten the length.

Hard areas to balance are those where you supply two fairways or lines of play—one for the long man and one for the shorter golfer. On these you can easily keep the poor driver on his own side, but often the fine hitter will try the other man's fairway. Traps beyond the reach of the short driver which do not trouble his average second, but which penalize the long driver, will answer the problem.

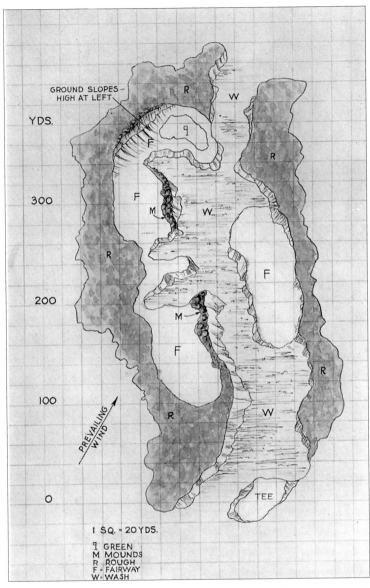

Double fairways built around a dry wash (on the principle of No. 8, Los Angeles Athletic).

Note that the hazards require players of different lengths to take certain lines and balance is maintained. On such holes one large tee is sufficient.

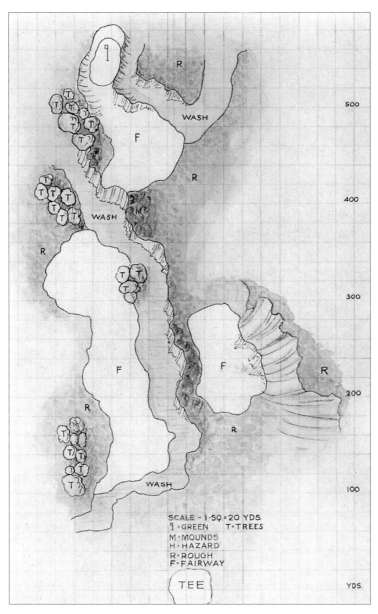

A short three shotter with an extra fairway at right for long drive, which gives a more advantageous position for second, but the long man may hit a long ball to the left fairway without being trapped. (From original drawing.)

When one comes to the areas of greens, the really difficult part of the proposition is faced, because greens are so much more significant in the play of the hole than any other equation; and there are so many things which affect the problem of the area of different greens, that the whole matter is most intricate. Here it is that the course builder must visualize with great accuracy the length of the stroke required, and the way various shots will act on reaching the green, and by foreseeing what the golfer and the golf ball will do, decide on the shape, extent and character of the green and its surroundings. He will give his opening, if any, the right width, and arrange for traps and fairways at the sides and beyond the green, as well as provide a green with necessary size and conformation for the reception of the ball.

While it is out of the question to make any arbitrary sizes for greens under the many varied conditions which will obtain, nevertheless, it is possible to give an idea of their correct dimensions by giving approximate measurements for their surfaces on flat holes. If these are used as a comparison, and the factors under any given condition considered in connection with them, it is believed that a guide will be supplied.

For a full wooden shot without carrying trap in front, a green should be not less than one hundred feet in length, with a minimum width of ninety feet, but one hundred and twenty-five feet for length, and one hundred feet for width would be better. The opening should equal this width; and where there is a carrying

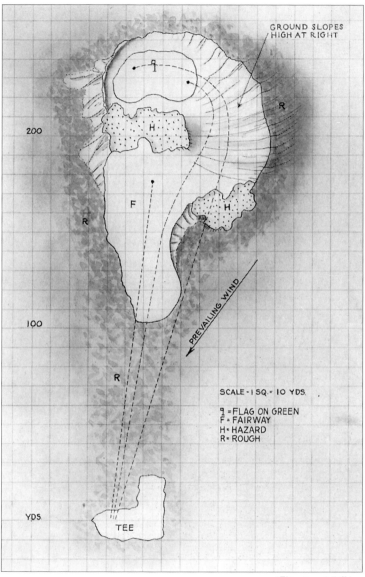

GROUND SLOPES
HIGH AT RIGHT

200

R

H

R

F

H

R

100

PREVAILING WIND

R

SCALE - 1 SQ. = 10 YDS.

⚑ = FLAG ON GREEN
F = FAIRWAY
H = HAZARD
R = ROUGH

YDS

TEE

(*Thomas and Bell.*)

No. 3, LOS ANGELES ATHLETIC.

A Redan which may be played three different ways. The short man goes to the left for safety. A slicer takes the central path and by accurate placement reaches the green without carry, the hill aiding him. The long man carries the right hand trap and is nursed by the slope to the green. The slope at right requires this green to be wide, not long. Note tee is made very large, and can be cut as desired.

trap and no opening, add fifty feet of fairway back of the green; the carrying trap should be fifty feet short of the green. For all openings, if the sides of the same are built up, and slope toward the center, the width may be reduced.

Where your approach to such a green for a full shot is either uphill or downhill, the conditions must be considered; and the size of the green, the size of the opening, the distance of the carrying trap, if any, from the green; and the amount of fairway beyond the green must be calculated for the reception of the shots which it will take care of. In making these computations one should provide for the shot of the long man played to reach the green and secure par; and also for the shot of the short man. It is the way the balance of area is arranged for golf shots that a hole is properly or improperly constructed, and the strategy of the same either a success or a failure.

Taking up the sizes of greens for flat conditions for shots shorter than a full wood (already given), the following areas are suggested as guides:

For a spoon shot or cleek, or a long iron to a green which is, roughly, from one hundred and eighty to two hundred yards, the minimum of the green should be ninety feet in depth, by eighty feet in width; but, preferably, it should be one hundred and ten feet by ninety feet; and carrying traps, if used, should be thirty feet short of the green, in which event give thirty feet of fairway behind green.

Greens built for the reception of a medium iron shot, the length of which is one hundred and sixty-five

Courtesy of Charles D. Willson.
The Rolyat.

(Stiles and Van Kleek.)

THIRD GREEN, PASADENA CLUB, ST. PETERSBURG, FLORIDA.

to one hundred and eighty yards, should be ninety feet in depth by seventy-five feet in width as a minimum—preferably, ninety-five by eighty-five feet; the carrying trap, if used, twenty feet short of the green, in which case give twenty feet of fairway behind green.

For greens to receive a jigger, mashie iron, or short iron, length from one hundred and fifty to one hundred and sixty-five yards, minimum size of the green should be eighty-five feet in depth by seventy feet in width—preferably, ninety by eighty feet; carrying trap, if used, fifteen feet short of the green, in which event give fifteen feet of fairway behind green.

Greens to receive long mashie shot, the length from one hundred and forty to one hundred and fifty yards, the minimum size of the green should be eighty feet in depth by sixty-five feet in width—preferably eighty-five by seventy-five feet; carrying trap, if used, ten feet short of the green, in which case give ten feet of fairway behind green.

For greens to receive long mashie niblick, length from one hundred and twenty-five to one hundred and forty yards, the minimum size of the green should be seventy-five feet in depth by sixty feet in width—preferably, eighty by seventy feet; the carrying trap, if used, five feet short of the green, in which case give five feet of fairway behind green.

For greens to receive a short mashie niblick, the length from one hundred to one hundred and twenty-five yards, the minimum size of the green should be seventy feet in depth by fifty-five feet in width—preferably, seventy-five by sixty feet; the carrying trap, if used, should be close to the side of the green with no fairway beyond.

Fairways beyond greens, and at their sides, must be supplied when needed.

Greens other than oval are prepared for particular shots, and the dimensions just presented are for ordinary and not special conditions. Note that it is much more difficult to build intricate greens and provide for all playing conditions than to construct average greens for average shots.

Undoubtedly, special strategy with originality is more interesting than more simple propositions. However, it is suggested that both be supplied for contrast and variety.

There are many combinations possible, and the areas suggested are given as a general guide; and, as noted repeatedly, are for flat or gently rolling surfaces, without distinct grades. It should be stated again, most emphatically, that any and all existing conditions which affect the shot, should affect the size of the green and its surroundings.

If the architect properly visualizes the way the golf ball will act, his green should retain the well-played shot, and the poor shot should either fall short of the green, or go beyond it, or to the sides, making a par more difficult.

It cannot be emphasized too strongly, that the area of the green, and all the factors of rough and hazard adjacent, must work into the strategy of the hole. The tee shot must require certain placements in areas of

Courtesy of Donald Ross.   *(Ross.)*
Bunker guarding a mashie-shot hole. Green artificially built on flat land. Dunedin Isles, Florida.

Photograph by Rau.   *(Wilson.)*
ELEVENTH, EAST COURSE, MERION, PA.
A fine pitch shot with proper green area.

proper surface, and the green must require more exact placements to areas of balanced surface.

In this connection, pitches should require distance rather than direction, because pitches are played by clubs with considerable loft, and shots from such clubs are more difficult to keep on the exact line than shots from clubs with less loft.

The running shots, on the contrary, are usually played from clubs with slight loft, and require direction rather than exact distance.

In conformity with this, pitch and run shots, which are approximately half way between the pitch shot and the running shot, should demand reasonable direction and reasonable distance.

For these reasons short, or fairly short-pitch shots, should have greens built for their reception which have little depth and extreme width, and a trap close in front of the green; while for running shots, the green with great depth and narrow width, with traps at the sides of the opening, is advisable. For the medium pitch and run the green with nearly equal width and depth is the requisite.

It will be seen from these suggestions that the guide for green surfaces is made not only for flat conditions, but also for the average medium high shot to the green; and that, where the architect forces the player to make a certain type of shot to a green, his green must conform in depth and width, and total surface to the shot exacted.

As a general consideration, it should be stated that where the natural rough is very severe, the fairway

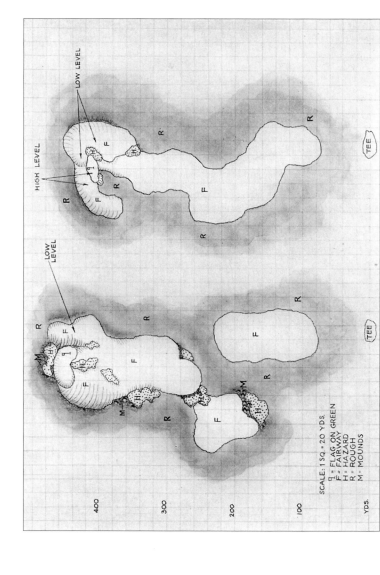

Greens raised above fairways on one side and level with them on the other supply attractive variation. Central entrances for third shot running approaches further diversify the play. Carrying hazards or placements may be used on drives, and either double fairways or dog-legs designed.

The suggestion at left is difficult for drive and easy on long man's second; the plan at right requires superlative second after driving placement. (From original drawing.)

may properly be made rather wider than is the usual rule, and that, for the same reason, the area of the green should be increased. Where rough is easy to play from, the fairway may be narrower. When little penalty is put upon the player in the rough adjacent to a green, that green may rightly be smaller.

Parallel fairways should have as great a width of rough as possible between them; and if only two are adjacent, the play should be forced away from the central rough as much as is practical.

Where the rough is severe, a narrow fairway without traps, and a green without fairway at the sides, is sometimes more difficult than stiff hazards and easy rough with broader fairway.

The area of rough should never be restricted between fairways and out of bounds.

Where a public street runs near the course passers-by must be protected from wild shots; and if adjacent property is likely to cause interference of any kind rough must be of sufficient width.

In considering area one must not neglect to make allowances for ground which floods, or which has poor underdrainage, because such territory is often out of play during rainy weather or in early spring.

Under such conditions many fairways are greatly improved by underdrainage and by protection from surface overflows.

Land which floods may often be guarded, and greens in such locations should be placed on the highest levels, or raised above low situations. On the other hand, certain ground cannot be made safe, and, as noted earlier in this text, land which floods badly should not be selected for golf courses.

Much damage may be done to the course by wash-outs; in some cases whole fairways have been lost and greens destroyed.

Where part of the property floods and the other portion is above storm water it is well to have a loop of holes in the low section, so that the high levels may be played as a unit during rainy weather.

Again, when high water is restricted in extent, the course may be planned so that overflow does not affect the play.

Many things enter into this problem; and local history and competent engineers should both be consulted on any location where this danger threatens.

The area problem is the question of balancing the entire course to the shots which it requires. The disposition, shape, and actual square yardage of tees, fairways, hazards, rough and greens, are all integral parts of the equation of golf ball placement.

The balance of area must be provided for with strict attention to detail.

Photograph by Rau.   (Heebner and Thomas.   Alterations by Deming.)

NINTH GREEN (A PITCH), WHITEMARSH, PENNSYLVANIA.

IX

ACTUAL CONSTRUCTION

IF YOUR framework and foundation have been worked out in accordance with the principles set forth in the foregoing chapters, you are now ready for actual construction.

It is necessary to clear the ground, to remove trees, or heavy brush, or rocks, and to have your fairways in shape for grading, to prepare the soil for seed and seeding.

In connection with such preparation the fairways should be most thoroughly free from anything which will interfere with the playing of shots. Another point often not considered is the fact that land adjacent to the fairways should, where possible, be prepared to some extent, so that the golfer may recover from wild shots which land outside the fairway.

At Pine Valley, for example, next the fairway there is a strip of varying width, usually from ten to twenty-five yards, where the rough is playable, and beyond, heavy undergrowth has been thinned.

Grading should next occupy your attention, and plans for all of it should be ready and passed upon, so that your working crews may proceed from one end of your course to the other in a sweeping advance. It should not be a question of going from No. 1 to No. 2, and so on. It should rather be a programme that takes in the construction of adjacent greens, fairways and hazards, and moves steadily across the property. In doing this see that a loop of nine holes may be played before the balance are ready.

Pipe line for water should be placed with the grading advance, and any planting of trees or shrubs be done after its completion, and water is obtainable.

Piping a golf course is an art in itself, involving questions of pressure and other technical matters which must be worked out by an expert. While it is not now customary in all parts of our country to water fairways, nevertheless most districts will eventually use sprinkling over their entire courses; certainly you should water your greens and tees.

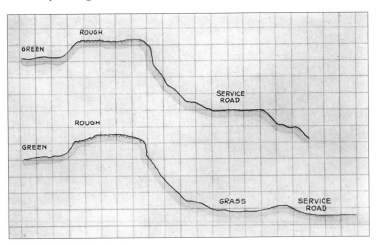

Upper outline from actual condition. A ball trickling over the edge runs down the bank and often goes through the road.

Lower, shows solution. By this plan balls which run over the edge are nearly all caught by the grass hollow below.

Courtesy L. A. Athletic Club.   *(Thomas and Bell.)*

CONSTRUCTION UNDER WAY ON THE COURSE OF LOS ANGELES ATHLETIC CLUB.
Note sand in traps before completion.

Photograph by Levick.   *(Wright.)*

FIFTH GREEN, ST. LOUIS COUNTRY CLUB, ST. LOUIS, MO.
Miss Collett putting in final, Women's Championship, 1925.
Courtesy of Golf Illustrated.

All grading which includes the making of tees, fairway rolls, hazards, greens and necessary drainage, must be entirely finished before seeding any unit.

In addition, roads for service through the grounds are very important; and these, and foot bridges, and other bridges must be built. Those used during construction should be planned to give access when the course is in play.

In years past hazards were made after the fairway was in grass, the theory being that they were often misplaced otherwise, and that the course should be tried before their final positions were chosen.

Nowadays, it is found more desirable, for many reasons, to do grading, including trapping, before

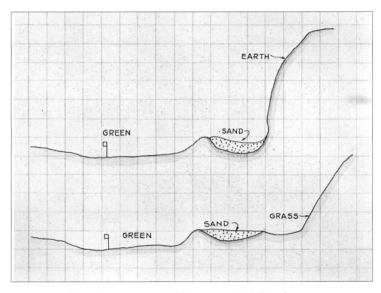

Above, improper way to build trap next to bank beyond green.
Below, proper method for same.

seeding, and the good sense of such practice is plainly apparent. First, it is a finished and not a patched job, and the drainage is more easily mapped as a whole, if done at one time. Sand may be placed on the ground as the hazards are built, and it is not necessary to bring this in afterwards. Most important of all, the new fairways will not be cut up, bruised and soiled by the

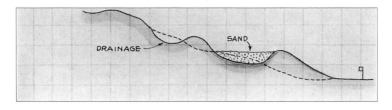

SHOTS AT RIGHT ANGLES TO CROSS SECTIONS.
Correct manner to trap fairly steep hill with drainage taken care of above. Dotted line shows original contour.

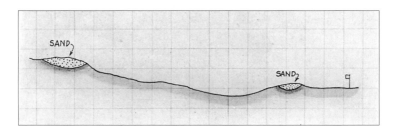

This drawing suggests sand for a lighter grade.

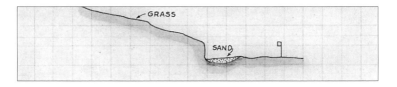

The wrong way to trap the bottom of a hillside—hazard receives drainage of hill and ball near bank is unfairly penalized.

Photograph by Black D.

(*Thomas and Bell.*)

SIXTH GREEN, LOS ANGELES ATHLETIC CLUB.

A pitch hole of 145 yards. Green after "O. K." and before seeding. Note large green divided by small trap into two compartments. Traps ready for sand. Sides of traps are built to portray erosion.

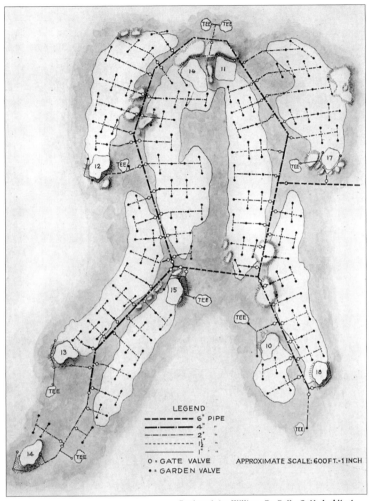

Designed by William P. Bell, Golf Architect.
WATER SYSTEM AT BAYSIDE, SAN DIEGO, CALIFORNIA.
Illustration shows complete piping for 9 holes of 18-hole course.

unavoidable tramping of teams, and the dragging of implements across them if hazards are made before seeding, while the completion of the course by one operation is economical, and to play it after it is finished more pleasing.

If change tees have been provided, and optional hazards with open fairways for the short player arranged, hazards will seldom be wrongly placed. Incidentally, it is much easier to fill up a hazard, or portion of a hazard, and call it ground under repair, than it is to construct new hazards.

When you come to the seeding of a course, you open the much-mooted question of the best varieties of grass. The most satisfactory grass for fairways and for greens is still the source of unending argument, and as important as the selection of the kind of grass, is the preparation of the seed bed to receive it; and this applies particularly to the seed bed for the green.

In olden times there was the "shot-gun green mixture," which contained different kinds of grass seed, on the theory that the one best suited to conditions thrived, and the others were crowded out, or died.

A very keen golfer of Philadelphia, a Mr. Taylor, who was generally known as "Efficiency Taylor," tested many varieties of seed in carefully prepared beds, subjecting the grass germinated to the extreme of dry heat without water, and of dampness without sun; and by these trials he contributed very valuable data.

Furthermore, the seed beds which he finally decided upon as the most nearly perfect, and the variety

Photograph Reproduction by Mills.   *(Bell.)*

EIGHTEENTH, CASTLEWOOD, NEAR OAKLAND, CALIFORNIA.

Courtesy of William P. Bell.

Photograph by Rau.   *(Macdonald.)*

SEVENTEENTH, NATIONAL COURSE, LONG ISLAND.

of grass which he considered gave best results, were used on some of the greens of the Sunnybrook Golf Club, near Philadelphia, and elsewhere. These seed beds were complicated, and "Outing Magazine" described them in a contemporary article.

Without going very deeply into the details of these greens, it should be said that their general principles were complete underdrainage, a heavy body of plant food in the form of organic manure, placed above the drainage; a sufficient amount of friable soil; that is, a composition of soil which would not pack and thereby restrict the growth of grass roots later on.

It would seem that these considerations must be supplied on clay courses, as in Taylor's construction, but where there is light, sandy loam, or sand, it is not always necessary to supply underdrainage; sometimes it is requisite to add heavier soil to retain moisture.

Recently I played over the Sunnybrook course, and found the greens there to be still in remarkably fine condition, their great virtue being that they did not dry out under heated circumstances and become hard; and that, in rainy weather, they were not too soggy.

The Department of Agriculture at Washington has established a Green Section for supplying accurate information to golf clubs throughout the country on the composition of greens, and also on their experiments in connection with different grasses. The short descriptions included herein concerning grasses are made as a sketch only and not to be considered in any way except as suggestions.

It is advised that those who are constructing new courses should take up the matter of seed beds and grasses with the Department of Agriculture, as this Department keeps thoroughly in touch with this changing situation, and will give full and complete information on the best methods for various parts of the country.

Creeping bent turf that has been mowed daily and frequently top dressed.
Courtesy of "The Bulletin" of the United States Golf Association, Green Section.

Creeping bent turf that has been mowed daily but not properly top dressed (i.e., top dressed infrequently).
Courtesy of "The Bulletin" of the United States Golf Association, Green Section.

The late Dr. Piper, of the Green Section noted, was in charge of the Golf Department of our Government, before his death, and his book, written in conjunction

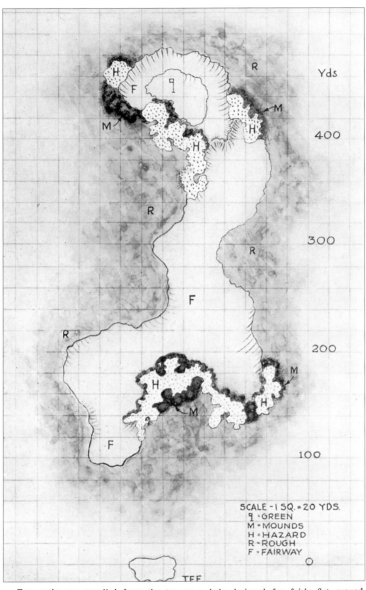

Two paths are supplied from the tee on a hole designed for fairly flat ground. A good type for all players. (From original drawing.)

with a fellow collaborator, and published by Macmillan under the title of "Turf for Golf Courses," gives very valuable data in connection with different grasses, means of identifying them, and conditions relative to their growth.

After the matter of drainage and retention of moisture, the main thing to remember in regard to a seed bed is that if there is only a thin layer of friable soil it will, undoubtedly, more easily become baked than a thicker layer, and under such conditions the green will not properly hold shots played upon it, but will become hard and compressed under the traffic it is subjected to. Not only will this occur nearly always on a clay course without underdrainage and depth of seed bed, but some types of silt have been known to become cement-like when subjected to watering, hot sun, and the tramping of many players.

Returning to the matter of different grasses, there have been a number of new developments since the old days, and we have gone through stages of using various grasses, and considering them as the best for our greens and fairways. Originally we used red top, blue grass and clover. Then we tried fescue and bent, the latter grass having for a time been planted by the vegetative or stolon method. Later on we reverted to the seed method with bent. We have also tried experiments with other varieties for the sides of our hazards and our rough.

Recently there has been a new bent developed by Dr. Carrier, of Oregon, which is known as Cocoos bent.

The old red top, and blue grass, and clover greens are undoubtedly inferior to the later developments. Bermuda, as a variety for greens, has lost its popularity, although there are some of these which gave very true putting surfaces, notably at the Los Angeles Country Club course; and these greens also contain indigenous grass of California, resembling Poa Annua.

At the Ojai Country Club in Ventura County, California, the greens are very fine. They are composed of fescue and red top, but they are somewhat inclined to be slow, although they seem well adapted to that climate of little frost in winter, and hot, dry summers; and, naturally, such greens are irrigated in that climate.

If the fairway is of Bermuda, and fescue is planted on the greens, it is invaded by Bermuda, and is also subject to mildew, especially in early fall.

If horse or cow manure is used on a green, it is very necessary to see that this manure does not contain ungerminated seeds of Bermuda, because under these conditions Bermuda will spread all over the green, and require most careful picking before it can be eradicated.

So far as may be decided, without a long test, the Cocoos bent is doing very well indeed; and as this is a creeping grass, it is more likely to ward off the incoming growth of other creepers, such as Bermuda. The bents are much superior for this reason. Metropolitan bent has been used with much success on some courses, but it would seem at this date that the Cocoos bent is very satisfactory.

The new La Cumbre course at Santa Barbara, the Bel-Air course near Los Angeles, and several other new courses, are giving fine results with this Cocoos bent, and if this grass continues to stand up under usage, it will be very popular.

Bermuda fairways are very good. The mat of grass they produce is velvety and quite thick, on account of which it makes a very attractive fairway covering; but its scope is restricted to climates with little frost, and it is a terrible invader of surface occupied by the finer putting green grasses.

The virtue of Bermuda is its ability to quickly heal scars made on it by the divots cut by descending golf clubs; but from late practice Bermuda is on the wane, except in the very hottest and driest conditions.

Meadow fescue has been used by the Los Angeles Municipal course on a terrain, some of which was originally pure, white sand, covered by a layer of good soil from four to six inches thick. Other parts of the course were heavy clay; and this grass has stood up well under the varied conditions, and very heavy traffic.

In certain places where greens have become hard, the use of a wire brush has been found beneficial each morning. This practice loosens the grass from the ground, and keeps it from being tramped flat, and a more receptive surface is afforded.

The fact that, after a green is seeded and completed, it is impossible to correct any errors to any extent without rebuilding, is evidence enough of the necessity of proper care in all matters pertaining to its grading,

Courtesy of Canadian Golfer.

SECOND GREEN, JASPER PARK, CANADA.

Wonderful scenery on a scale which demands a large hazard.

(Thompson.)

its drainage, its seed bed, and the kind of grass planted, all of which must be perfect in order that the green plays properly. Not only are changes to greens most expensive, but, furthermore, the play of that hole is ruined, because a temporary green usually plays short of the regular one while it is undergoing changes; takes away from the playing value of the hole, and is very inferior as a putting surface.

Fairways are not hard to get in shape; hazards may be changed; tees easily rebuilt or moved at reasonable expense, and without affecting the play to an unfortunate degree; but the green cannot be changed without much trouble, expense and irritation.

The following methods are used in the preparation of fairways and greens by the golf architect, William P. Bell, with whom I have had the pleasure of working in the building of courses. He advises that his methods are at this date in conformity with those suggested by the Green Section of the Department of Agriculture.

Preparing the Seed Bed for Fairways

"After the ground is ploughed, use a spike harrow and roller, or drag many times until there is a fine, mellow layer at least two to three inches deep. Make sure that there are no hollows or sharp ridges, as these would interfere with the mowing after the grass is up.

Sowing the Seed

"Best results are obtained by using the wheelbarrow type of seeder, sowing half of the seed lengthwise of the fairway and then sowing the other half crossways of the fairway. After this is done, use a very light smoothing harrow with the teeth slanting well backward; then finish off with a roller or very light board drag, or slab.

PREPARING THE SEED BED FOR GREENS

"The top six inches of a putting green surface should be composed of a good sandy loam, and at least two inches of this top should be put through a half-inch mesh screen so as to eliminate all rocks or roots, and thus make it possible to make a very smooth-finished surface. The preparation of a putting-green seed bed is exactly the same whether seed is to be sown or the green planted to bent stolons. If seed is to be sown, it should be raked in very lightly and then rolled with a light roller; it is then ready for the watering, which should be done with a fine nozzle hand sprinkler until the grass is well established. When the grass is about three weeks old, it is time to start to top dress. Best results are obtained by using a top dressing composed of one part loam, one part sand, and one part well-rotted manure or peat humus. This can be applied about one-eighth to one-quarter of an inch thick every two weeks until a very even putting surface has been established. This mixture not only trues up the putting surface, but it absorbs water readily, and will not bake, thereby making an ideal surface to hold a pitch shot."

As a matter of information, the cost of a golf course is given in our text, but it will be understood that many

Photograph by Collinge.

SEVENTEENTH GREEN, 95 YARDS, LA CUMBRE, SANTA BARBARA, CALIFORNIA.
Cut out of the slope; nearly flat for pitches, and oriented by sand and broken outlines.

(Thomas and Bell.)

things will affect an estimate for such work—the cost of clearing different kinds of country will vary; the amounts necessary to drain the course, and to install the pipe lines, are not fixed by any manner of means. The amount of earth which it is necessary to move affects the figures and it will be easily realized that many factors change the totals. Underdrainage on a heavy clay runs up to $10,000. However, the amounts given are those for an average course in California.

Clearing brush, trees, blasting rock, carrying sand and other necessary hauling............$ 4,000.00

Grading of each hole, which includes the tee, traps, green, contours, covering hollows, over average ground at $1,000.00 a hole 18,000.00

Water system—The newest is hoseless on the fairways, with hose on the greens, because no system except hose has yet been worked out which is flexible enough for green watering, and which does not interfere with the play. The water system would include ditching not including rocky ground; the laying of the pipe, cost of the pipe itself, its fittings, and the back filling or covering of the pipe; the sprinklers and their fittings...................... 24,000.00

Bent seed or bent stolons cost about $100.00 for 7,000 square feet, which would be an average green surface for 18 holes, say -- 2,000.00

Carried forward...$48,000.00

Brought forward..$48,000.00

Sowing of the fairways with whatever fairway grasses were used (Bermuda would
be about one-half the cost)........................   4,000.00

Labor of watering the course for six months,
cutting, care of greens and fairways, top
dressing, fertilizing for the same period;
and other such necessary work as rock
picking, weeding; about............................   20,000.00

Sand for the traps for an inland course not
over 4,000.00
                                                         _____
                                                         $76,000.00
                                                         _____

Such expenses would not include bridges, or
any necessary grading of roads. Equip-
ment of the best and most up-to-date
character would approximate an outside
figure of...$ 5,000.00
and all the above estimates are made for
an 18-hole course.

In California districts, where the course is played
for the entire year, and where it is necessary to irrigate
constantly during seven months of this period, and at
intervals during the other five months, varying with
the rainfall, the upkeep on a course of 6,500 yards,
which is kept up in the most careful manner, runs
from $25,000.00 to $30,000.00 a year as a minimum.

The average cost for ordinary labor on such a
course is placed at from $4.00 to $4.50 a day; and,
roughly speaking, it should take 20 men to care for
the average 18-hole course, and care for it properly.

Courtesy of Los Angeles Athletic Club.   *(Thomas and Bell.)*

A PIECE OF GROUND IN THE ROUGH.

Courtesy of Los Angeles Athletic Club.   *(Thomas and Bell.)*

THE SAME GROUND AFTER CONSTRUCTION.

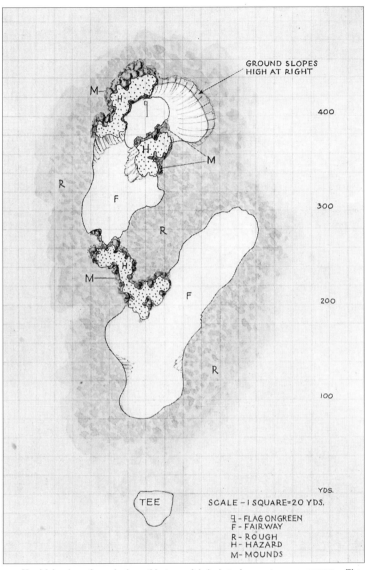

GROUND SLOPES
HIGH AT RIGHT

400

300

200

100

YDS.

TEE

SCALE – 1 SQUARE = 20 YDS.

⚑ – FLAG ON GREEN
F – FAIRWAY
R – ROUGH
H – HAZARD
M – MOUNDS

No driving hazard required on this type of hole but placement very necessary. The second shot may be played in various ways. (From original drawing.)

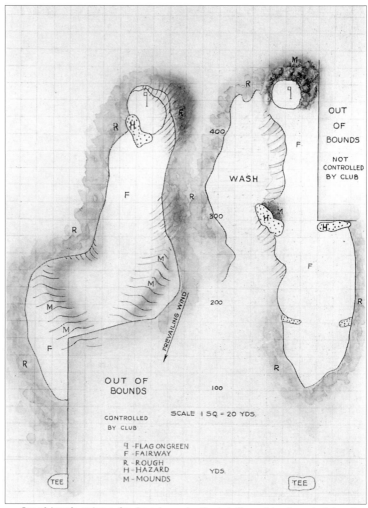

Out of bounds makes a fine hazard occasionally, but, if possible, the out of bounds should be controlled by club. Approximate sketches of two existing holes.

In the moving of your earth, extreme care must be used to finish the green with top soil, not sub soil, even if you are going to add other soil to secure a proper seed bed. This also applies to tees.

As your construction advances, your work must be constantly supervised, and the O. K. of your architect insisted upon before any green is seeded. It is necessary that contours should be checked, so that there is no possibility of the sinking of any part of a green, mounds, and so forth; and that all raised portions have been solidly packed, for it is remarkable how rain will shrink rolls if they are not carefully made. When such an event takes place, the appearance is nothing like that desired.

Tees will cause trouble if the lines which orient them to the player do not point in the direction of the tee shot. Before tees were made part of the fairway, and when their shapes were square and not suited to the surrounding terrain, it was the custom to place them by use of a large T square, so that their straight side lines pointed properly, for if these lines pointed in a wrong direction, or the straight front of the tee was not at right angles to the line of play, it was found that the players had difficulty in keeping direction.

More recently, since tees were made of various shapes and allowed to be part of the contour, such precautions are not so necessary; but, nevertheless, a curving line which is nearly straight, and which runs along the side of a tee and points in some other direction than the right one for the shot from that tee, will affect the play adversely; and where lines are made with the mower, they will affect the direction of the tee shot.

Lines separating fairway and rough should be sketched out in advance by the architect, staked on the ground for the first cuttings of the grass, and can afterwards be changed as found necessary.

Again and again, during course construction, I have been asked to let some employee of a club carry out the work, and whenever I have acceded to such requests, I have had the greatest difficulty in carrying out my plans properly. This is not intended in any way to reflect on the men who have done this work, but is rather to avoid subjecting them to a task for which they are not qualified, and which it is unfair to ask them to do.

No matter how good a man is for supervising a course, he may not have the golfing knowledge or the artistic sense, or the engineering education to carry out golf-course construction. The golf architect should be made responsible for contours; for every detail in the construction of the course. His contract should be made so that he either supervises this work himself, or supplies a competent foreman, who is responsible in his absence. In this latter event, the architect should inspect the job a stated number of times. You may spend more money by using his men than by trying to get him to work with yours at the time of the building, but eventually you will save if you make him entirely responsible, and have his O. K., especially before any seeding is done.

Courtesy A. W. Tillinghast.

(*Tillinghast.*)

FOURTH GREEN, 115 YARDS, BALTUSROL, NEW JERSEY.

Fine construction of artificial water hazard. Picture shows Robert Jones, American and British Open Champion, playing during 1926 Amateur Championship.

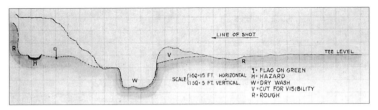

SHOTS INTO HILLSIDES.
Upper line shows original contours. Dotted line portrays finished contours. Sketch made from No. 17, Los Angeles Country Club, North Course. This green is illustrated elsewhere by photographs.

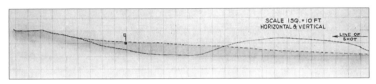

Black line shows contour which makes a pocket and a blind green. Dotted line shows drainage established and blindness gone. Such cuts and fills are often used on easily-worked soil.

After the plan of the course is accepted, do not change it and hamper the architect by letting your Green Committee, or any one else, supervise the work and take responsibility away from the architect, who may very properly say afterwards that errors which

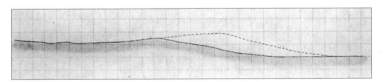

The continuation of a grade to secure distance. This requires an expensive fill.

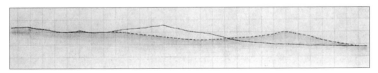

Below is a better solution where the cut makes fill and gives greater distance. Dotted lines are finished levels in both outlines.

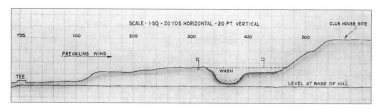

Approximate section of Eighteenth, on Los Angeles Athletic Club course. Wash was filled by soil taken from hill at right and greater length secured. Drainage was cared for by piping.

cropped out in the construction were caused by the men whom you had placed in charge.

By all means have the work watched, but make the architect responsible. There are some Green Committees who can build a golf course; there are many more who cannot do so.

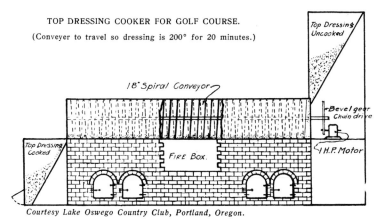

Courtesy Lake Oswego Country Club, Portland, Oregon.

In top dressing, where seeds of weeds or coarse grasses are found in soil used, a roasting furnace is advantageous; but such practice kills other life in soil and fertilization must be used on green. When peat moss or humus is used no seeds are present. Top dressing should not be done while natural seeds may be blown or carried to green.

X

REMODELING OLD COURSES

THE REBUILDING of courses is often severely criticised, and in many cases such censure is deserved; but it is well to remember that the gradual and continued improvement of golf courses has been brought about not only by the natural betterment of golf construction, but because of the increased efficiency of the golf ball, the playing value of which is more perfect, particularly with regard to its distance.

The advance in golf architecture, while progressing slowly, has, nevertheless, gone forward like other things, and lately the new handling of grasses and new varieties of grasses have also affected the situation. For these reasons, courses which were built some years ago cannot be expected to rank with the latest construction work. Therefore, there is often good reason for changes without censure to plans originally mapped out, and which produced the existing layout. On the other hand, there are courses which have not been properly constructed, and on which the strategy is not good. Furthermore, a club may decide to increase its playing arrangement from 18 to 36 holes.

Under some circumstances, there is the necessity of continuing play during the period of change; and with the aid of temporary greens and tees this may generally be accomplished. Ofttimes a new loop of holes constructed over new territory will take the place of other parts of the course to be changed.

Present-day methods entail a different type of architecture to that employed several years ago in a great many cases, although often the old holes may be remodelled without much expense, and thereby fit in properly with the new parts.

It is possible to add acreage to a congested tract, and improve the old ground by lessening the number of holes thereon, and secure additional character over them, possibly by dodging hills, lengthening holes which are too short, and by various means increasing the total yardage, if such is desired.

These problems are very confusing. It is really more difficult to reconstruct an old course than to lay out a new one, because the question frequently arises as to what should be discarded and what retained. One feels that every time one eliminates something, it may be possible that sufficient value, over and above what exists, is not obtained in the new construction. Very few of the old holes can be played as they stand, but undoubtedly the greater part of their fairways are valuable, and only the very finest of them should be kept intact.

Two courses which I helped to remodel, stand out as very different propositions. One was increased from 18 to 36 holes, and what was done may be a useful guide in connection with others considering the same kind of change.

In the particular case involved, we improved the first of one of the nines, using six of the old greens

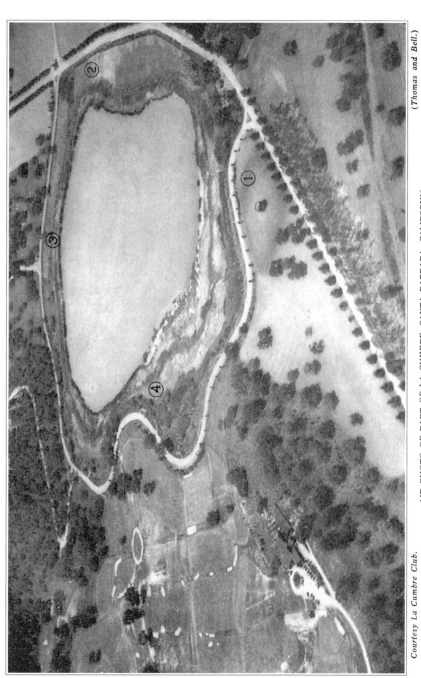

Courtesy La Cumbre Club. AIR PHOTO OF PART OF LA CUMBRE, SANTA BARBARA, CALIFORNIA. (*Thomas and Bell.*)

Before reconstruction. Numerals in circles show positions of new greens. (Holes 2, 3 and 4 are illustrated by drawing or photo in this text.) Clubhouse in left foreground.

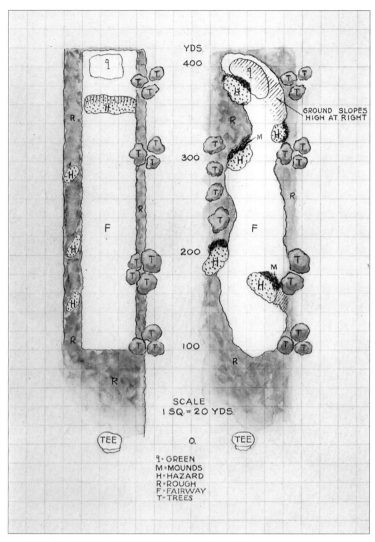

YDS.
400

300

200

100

GROUND SLOPES
HIGH AT RIGHT

SCALE
1 SQ. = 20 YDS.

TEE

O.

TEE

9 = GREEN
M = MOUNDS
H = HAZARD
R = ROUGH
F = FAIRWAY
T = TREES

At the left, a sketch of an old hole played about 1900.

At the left of the fairway is 20 yards of rough, beyond which is an adjacent fairway. At the right is out of bounds. The faults from a beauty standpoint are the straight lines; from a utility standpoint the lack of any character or of any placement required.

At the right is a solution of this hole, which gives strategy and variation. The drive must be placed.

and building three new ones in slightly different locations; but with minor exceptions the fairways remained exactly as they were. We then added an entirely new nine to this remodelled nine, and had, as a result, a complete eighteen with No. 1 tee and No. 18 green close to the clubhouse; and No. 9 green and No. 10 tee within a reasonable distance—roughly speaking, about 250 yards. In other words, we originally had two nines going out from the clubhouse site, and we developed two eighteens from the two nines, adding holes to each of the original nines. On the second nine so increased we kept No. 10; No. 12 and No. 13 with new greens, and No. 16 from a new tee; No. 17 and No. 18 as they were with some improvements. We found it expedient to eliminate No. 11, No. 14 and No. 15, and we constructed twelve new holes which fitted in with the six retained and made the other eighteen.

On the second course we had tees No. 1 and No. 10, and greens No. 9 and No. 18 adjacent to the clubhouse; and as the clubhouse was situated on the western boundary of the property, these six starting places close to it, and two starting places within 250 yards of it, were considered a good solution.

On the other proposition noted, the problem was the reconstruction of an 18-hole course, where there was entirely too much hill climbing, a lot of parallel fairways and too many short two-shot holes.

In order to work out this matter satisfactorily, we built four complete new fairways and greens, and part of a fifth fairway and its new green. We used nearly

Courtesy Country Club Magazine.   *(Thomas and Bell.)*

TWELFTH, 178 YARDS, LA CUMBRE, SANTA BARBARA, CALIFORNIA.

A reconstructed green.

all of the old fairways for the reception of 13 holes. In other words, we placed 13 units where there were originally 18, although, of course, all of the ground was not utilized in exactly the same way.

Of the old greens we kept only six, some of which we used with entirely different fairways, but all will eventually be remodelled or changed to some extent.

It will, therefore, be seen that very little was used of the old course, except the fairways; that practically an absolutely new course was constructed, and undoubtedly it was a vast improvement over the original holes. Such a reconstruction, where there is congestion, is a very different matter to changes in trapping, and other minor improvements on a course which has ample room. The latter undertaking is, of course, very much less expensive. It is as necessary to design such changes with great exactness as it is to plan a new course, and there is more chance of criticism in this work, although, personally, I rather enjoy bettering by minor changes; but the revamping of a course is much harder than the building of a new one.

In the remodelling of a course, the architect must be in complete sympathy with the Chairman of the Green Committee, and the policies of the club. He must approve of what is to be done before he can properly execute the wishes of the organization. When this cooperation exists, the work is a pleasure, and I have been fortunate in having been associated with Chairmen who knew golf and who were of the greatest assistance. On one of the last courses which I helped to reconstruct, I considered the Chairman had the utmost understanding of golf architecture, and the result was very successful.

When there is adverse criticism in rebuilding a course, it usually occurs when the work is undertaken by the man who formerly looked after the upkeep, and nearly always such workers are unable to understand the difference between their previous jobs of upkeep and their new ones of construction, even though they have done some little work in the making of traps and minor alterations.

It is very difficult for the architect to produce the same results with unskilled labor, as he is accustomed to create with men who understand his methods, and have produced former conceptions.

Reconstruction should be handled by the same type of labor which builds courses, and if the architect cannot have the construction men who have worked with him before, or others whom he can depend upon to carry out his plans, it would be better not to attempt the work. New traps and new tees are one thing, the proper moulding of greens an entirely different matter.

Therefore, do not try reconstruction without expert advice, and without giving your expert a proper chance to produce what both you and he desire.

Frequently it would be wise for an organization to consider the sale of the property, and the purchasing of a new tract, where an up-to-date course can be built, rather than to attempt the reconstruction of an old course, especially if such is not situated on terrain which will give the most advantageous results.

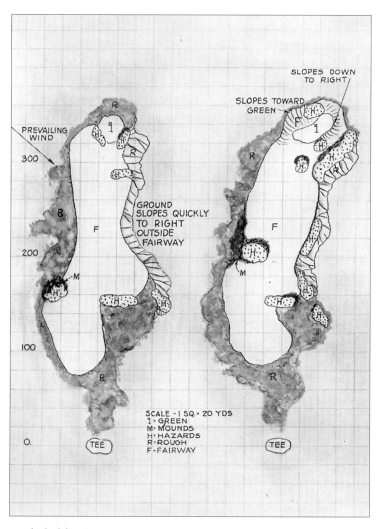

At the left, a hole with small green to require accurate play for pars—green trapped for same reason; the balance of green entrance and other areas make this a good hole for long and fairly long players, but exact heavy penalties from average golfers.

If hole was given long narrow green with new traps to require perfect play for long man's pars and slope at its left to aid short players, it would be a better hole. (From original drawing.)

Nevertheless, on numerous occasions I have endeavored to bring this opinion before committees of clubs, and found it very hard to impress them with the hopelessness of reconstructing a course of the highest character from mediocre possibilities.

If the proposition is for but a small membership, and great length is not desired, an old course, unless on very bad ground, should be reconstructed with success.

However, every problem is different, and must be solved to the satisfaction of those who own the property, and the architect must look at their point of view; but on the other hand, he should present to them what they will secure if they go ahead with remodeling.

While it is necessary in the remaking of old-fashioned courses to remodel, this should not be done so that the membership of a course, which has had rather easy play, will be under the necessity of making long carries from tees and to greens on the new layout, unless such changes are thoroughly understood. The theories for the building of a new course apply with equal force to the remade proposition.

As an example to emphasize the inadvisability of rebuilding many courses on which such work is contemplated, the proposition to rebuild a course was recently considered, where the land in question had quadrupled in value above its cost. This tract was of scant acreage, and without any real merit on any of its holes either in design or construction. The opportunity offered could never produce a truly first-class test.

Courtesy of Golf Illustrated.   *(Ross.)*

BROADMOOR GOLF COURSE, COLORADO SPRINGS.

Courtesy of Golf Illustrated.   *(Ross.)*

NINTH GREEN, ST. AUGUSTINE, FLORIDA.

In such a situation it would seem most advisable for the architect to advocate strongly the purchase of new property, because in addition to the existing situation, the value of the ground will eventually lead to extremely high taxes, which will almost prohibit the use of this property for golf purposes. If the club waits until that time before securing a new home, land which might earlier have been bought at reasonable prices will, in its turn, have increased in value. Perhaps this is the strongest argument against rebuilding of courses which can only have a few years of life on account of the improvement in property values.

In the case of the Merion Cricket Club, in Philadelphia, it was possible to give up the old golf course, keep the old clubhouse, tennis courts, and other necessary land for community club and meeting places, and to build first one golf course of 18 holes, and eventually a second course of 18 holes on other pieces of property further out in the country, where courses were secured which were infinitely superior in every way to the old one. This experience has been duplicated in many cases.

From the writer's experience, he believes that the great majority of golfers desire a course which requires accurate and skillful play for the producing of par figures, and the strategy which has been outlined in this book has been evolved gradually not only from the improvement of our old courses, but by the production of the new ones. It is not in any way the theory of any one man, but rather the solution which has been attained by general custom, has been gradually evolved, and which has been tested in the fire of usage.

It is true that various authorities hold somewhat different theories on golf construction; nevertheless, most of them agree on the main points.

Often a trap may be placed about which there is much comment when it first appears; but if that particular hazard is fair, if it gives an option to the high handicap man, such criticism will gradually die out, and eventually it will be commended. This applies most especially to the trapping of old holes, where the players are used to certain conditions, and where the new arrangement at first causes adverse criticism.

On a trap which I recently constructed, one player objected to it because he said: "If I make a bad drive, I cannot get on the green on my second shot." When everybody roared with laughter, it was realized that this very feature was the one which made the trap necessary and valuable.

Years ago there was a very canny Green Chairman, who placed piles of sand in the positions on his fairways where he proposed to make new traps, and after he had noted the result, on the play of the hole, and given the members a chance to express their opinions, he either built the hazards, or took away the sand; and it was really quite surprising to note how many times he removed the sand, which shows the futility of placing new traps on old holes, unless there is a crying need for their presence.

The most necessary places for new traps are on courses where there is congestion, particularly where

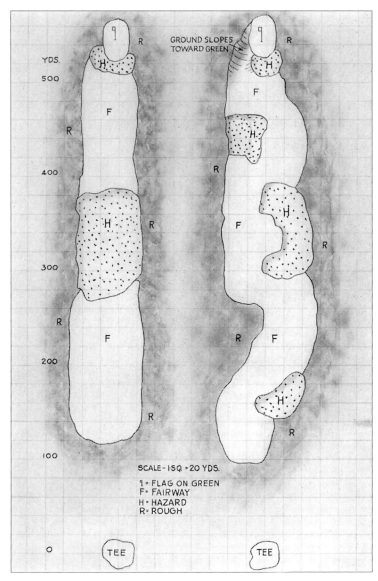

At the left, compulsory carries. The average man must play short on his second; the fine golfer has a splendid test of length but no placement.

At the right, the traps require placement on both drive and second with a safe line of play for all golfers, and little loss in par value for the long man; yet with a narrow opening to the green for accurate thirds of short players.

Diagram at left is rough copy of principle employed on well-known courses some years ago—that at right, more recent strategy with less hardship.

there is danger; and when this has been located and recognized, it is imperative for those in charge to make such changes, and to give protection that will remove the peril.

In reconstructing Bermuda courses, great care must be used to eradicate the Bermuda from the soil below the position of new greens, otherwise it will come up through a green of newly-sown seed; but if the green is sodded with thin Cocoos sod, this danger is not so likely. It is, nevertheless, safer in any event to excavate the earth to a depth not less than eighteen inches, and then to refill with new and clean earth. This has been done with success on seeded greens, and the reason that eighteen inches is all that is necessary to excavate is that, while the fibrous feeding roots of Bermuda cut down to a greater depth, such roots will not send up runners or shoots. The heavy roots which run down to a lesser depth are the ones which must be eradicated. While sodded greens render the danger of Bermuda appearing from below much less, it should be noted that greens sowed to stolons are equally vulnerable with greens sowed to seed; there is practically no difference in their ability to resist the Bermuda from below.

Unless the greatest care is exercised, fescue greens become so invaded by other growth that it is generally necessary to reconstruct them after a very few years. There are not many places where such care has been maintained, perhaps the most notable example in the West being at the Wilshire Country Club, where, by the most scientific and careful weeding, the greens have been kept free from other growth.

FIFTH GREEN, MIAMI BEACH, FLORIDA.

GENERAL VIEW, SAN PEDRO COURSE, CALIFORNIA.

It would seem essential that every golf course should have its own nursery of bent grass, so that if greens do become invaded, it will be possible, by cutting the nursery sod very thin—approximately one inch in thickness—and in long strips, to place it on the prepared surface of the green without keeping the same out of play for more than a couple of weeks. In other words, this thin-cut sod really acts like stolons, but its knitting is attained more rapidly than their growth.

If the soil on your course has considerable clay in it, it would be well to use a layer of sandy loam on top for the sowing of seed in the nursery for grass to be used in transplanting, because a sandy sod will move much more easily than the clay sod, and without cracking; it will also be a better sod for your green.

Surface drainage and underdrainage are serious problems in the reconstruction of old courses.

XI

ARBITRARY VALUES

PAR IS a somewhat arbitrary ruling for determining the proper number of strokes in perfect play, and par has distance as its main measure.

Par allows two putts to every green, and is divided by yardage as follows:

Holes up to and including 250 yards, are par 3; from 251 to 445 yards inclusive, par 4; from 446 to 600 yards inclusive, par 5; above 600 yards, par 6.

This means that in perfect play a golfer should reach a distance up to 250 yards in one stroke from the tee, and with his two putts make a three on a hole of such length. He should negotiate a distance of from 251 to 445 yards in two strokes, and with his two putts secure a par 4. From 446 to 600 yards he should cover the ground in three strokes, and with his two putts register a par 5. Anything over 600 yards he should reach in four efforts, and with his two putts make a par 6, although, as a matter of fact, par 6 holes are seldom supplied. This ruling, however, is not entirely arbitrary, as the U. S. G. A. definitions of par allow the various clubs to change par to conform to local conditions, suggesting that when yardage for any par differs from the schedule supplied, reasons for such change should be explained on the score card, under local rules.

Photograph by Martin. (*Thomas and Bell.*)

ELEVENTH, 350 YARDS, OJAI, CALIFORNIA.

A natural contour for a pitch.

Theoretically, par should be approximately equal on all holes; that is to say, it should be as difficult to score a 3 on a three-par hole, as it should be to score a 4 on a four-par hole, or a 5 on a five-par hole; also that pars requiring the same number of strokes should be of nearly equal value. Practically, this is not the case, mainly because length cannot be overcome as easily as placement under existing conditions.

It is easier for a long man to lay his short iron on any ordinary green than to play a longer shot to a somewhat larger green. It is still easier for him to lay his short mashie niblick dead for a three, or one under par on a short two shotter, than to lay his brassie, or long iron, close to the pin on a long two shotter. On one shotters the same holds true.

Correspondingly, it is easier for the short man to place his second shot on a short two shotter on the green, and go down in two putts, than to lay his third shot dead and go down in one putt on a long two shotter, where he cannot possibly reach the green in two strokes. Of course, it is much simpler for him to reach the green on a short one shotter and secure his par, than it is for him to lay a second dead, or go down in one putt on a long one shotter, which he cannot hope to reach with his longest stroke.

Most players get fewer birdies on long two shotters than on short two shotters and fewer on long one shotters than short one shotters.

Therefore, pars of different holes are not of equal value.

It would be impossible to arrange for this unless the greens on short holes were made so small and difficult for the long player, that the shot to them would equal in skill the longer shot made on long holes. If this were done, it would readily be understood that the greens would be so difficult for the short player that they would be unfair. For this reason it is necessary to make the greens on many holes easier than they should be for the reception of the play of the long hitter, who has a short shot to them.

Nevertheless, it is easy to compute the par of all holes but the longest one shotters and the longest two shotters. There is little argument except on these distances, although the values of the pars are more or less unequal.

The spirit of par, worked out by schedule, requires a certain distance to be negotiated by the player, and two putts added to such distance to secure the par; but it is often the case that, owing to playing conditions, actual yardage should not decide the par. Too often the selection of par on various courses is decided, so that the par of the course should be increased to a desired ideal, rather than the accurate par given.

In constructing holes the matter of par should be carefully considered, and the distances and their pars arranged in accordance with the true spirit of par, rather than to pad the course for its yardage or its par; and nothing but the value of the distance, as affected by average playing conditions, should decide the par.

It is better to have a shorter hole with a par of real value, than a longer one to pad yardage with an

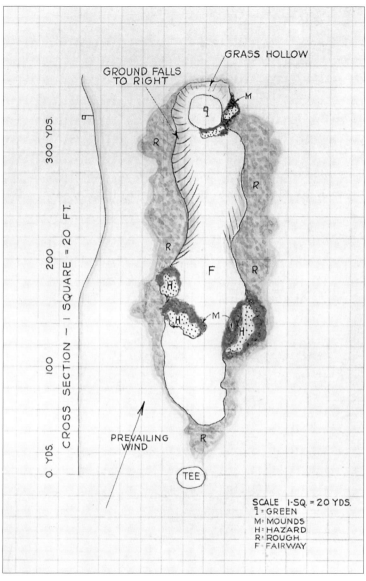

GRASS HOLLOW

GROUND FALLS TO RIGHT

M

q

R

R

R

R

F

R

H

H

M

H

PREVAILING WIND

R

TEE

300 YDS.

200

100

0. YDS.

CROSS SECTION — I SQUARE = 20 FT.

SCALE 1-SQ. = 20 YDS.
q = GREEN
M = MOUNDS
H = HAZARD
R = ROUGH
F = FAIRWAY

Memory outline of an existing 330-yard hole which is a ridiculously easy par for the ordinary golfer, and an easy chance for a birdie by the scratch player.

The prevailing wind and downhill grade aid the ball, and an average 200-yard shot goes within a few yards of the green.

unfair par.   For example, up to 250 yards is par 3;
yet no one should put in a 250-yard hole up a steep
hill, and call it a par 3, because it would play longer
than that yardage, as no one is expected to go over
250 yards for perfect play, and such effort would not
reach uphill for the same distance.   It is much better
to shorten the hole so that it would play an average
250 yards, be the distance as low as 200 yards.   You
would thereby provide a suitable test of play, and have
an honest par with unpadded yardage.

Should a hole be downhill, and of 275 or even 300
yards, and could it be reached by a shot of 250-yard
value, on level ground, it should be par 3 rather than
par 4.   On such a hole make a very large green for
a running shot, with no close carrying traps; and place
fairway beyond and at its sides.

Therefore, you must arrange your pars for the
exact playing value of your holes.   Your yardage is
secondary, and the illustrations for long one shotters
apply equally to long two shotters.

Upgrades, prevailing adverse winds, sandy soils,
all affect the estimate of pars, and these fundamentals
should be carefully considered as requiring less length
for pars, just as downgrades, prevailing following
winds and fast ground, should demand greater length
for pars.

In order to create a fitting par for short two
shotters, it has been advocated that as they are easier
than long two shotters, there should be a par value
of $3\frac{1}{2}$ for such holes; and for the same reason a value
of $4\frac{1}{2}$ for holes with average playing distance of from

446 to 500 yards. This suggestion, undoubtedly, has merit, but under existing arbitrary values, and without other changes, the correct estimate of pars may be obtained by constructing the holes for definite shots, and, where possible, avoiding the building of holes on which the par cannot be made legitimate, although it will be impossible to do more than secure reasonably accurate values for existing average conditions.

Do not add yardage for a greater par unless character and a fair test is obtained; and do not decrease yardage in one place to increase par in another place, if you lose character, par value, or diversity. Your holes should be values mapped in connection with your ground demands, not juggled yardage or par without quality or variation.

Let us drop par values for a moment and consider them later from another angle, which cannot be clearly understood unless we take up the very perplexing question of the value of the putting stroke.

Much has been said regarding the too great value of the putter. It has been suggested that the cups on the greens be made larger so that putting would be easier, but this has never met with enough favor for a change, although a step in that direction is noted in the matter of the placement of our cups in easy locations on the greens, especially in medal tournaments. Even on short two shotters some well-known players object to cups in places requiring very exact positions by drive; and second, for the scoring of par or the chance of a birdie. It is now the general custom to place the positions of the cups, in championship medal competitions, on flat ground on the green, or else in locations where the surrounding contours nurse the ball toward the hole.

Whenever a cup is located on any ground which approaches the formation of a ridge, or is part of a roll, especially where the ground falls away from the cup on any side, there is a general complaint against such placement, although more skill would be required in making putts under those conditions. All this goes to show that putting has too great a value, and that the best players object to increasing it by making putting harder than seems to them necessary.

As has already been stated, half the shots of par golf are putts—undoubtedly too great a proportion.

Advocates of greens without grades, which accelerate the speed of the ball, are at heart actuated by the tremendous value of the putt. Nevertheless, it seems a poor way out of the difficulty to eliminate our putting skill by requiring golfers to play on greens without ridges and grades; yet, if we do build greens with rolling contours, we further enhance the top heavy valued putter; and to cut out the character and attractiveness of rolling greens is beyond thought.

A new theory which has been advanced is the simplest and most effective solution in the world, and is attained by cutting down the value of the putt, something which many desire. This is done by reducing each stroke of the putter from the value of one stroke to the value of half a stroke, and leaving every other club's stroke as at present with a value of one

(Ross.)
VIEW AT BEL-AIR COUNTRY CLUB, FLORIDA.

(Ross.)
SAND TRAP, EIGHTEENTH HOLE, No. 2 COURSE, PINEHURST, N. C.

stroke. By "putting strokes" is meant any stroke on the cut surface of the putting green.

This would appear to give putting sufficient value, for on a par of 18 holes, under the new system, 36 putts, or two putts to a green, instead of having a value of 36 strokes, would have a value of 18 strokes, and the total number of par strokes for the round would be 54 instead of 72, which would give the putter a value of about 33⅓ per cent of the total number of strokes in the round, instead of 50 per cent as at present. No other club in the bag would count for as much.

Consider for a moment what would happen under this scoring system. The man who misses his drive, misses his second, gets on the green on his third, and goes down in one putt, would, under this method, take three and a half strokes. The man who was playing against him, and who hit a good drive, a good second, and went down in two putts, would score three strokes and win the hole, as he deserves to win it, because he has made no mistake; and the other man has not played perfectly.

Further, the player who, by two fine strokes, reached the large green of a long two shotter, where he was a considerable distance from the hole, and who took three putts to go down, would take three and a half strokes; and his opponent, who took three strokes to the green, and then two putts, would score four strokes. The first player, who had made two very fine shots, and really not made a bad stroke on the green— because no one can be expected to lay extremely long putts dead at all times, especially if greens are rolling

—would rightfully win the hole, as the second man has, undoubtedly, played an imperfect shot, and has been unable in three strokes to get near enough to the hole to go down in one putt, having made no real recovery.

Under the old system the hole would be halved in five, which does not seem fair to the man who has practically made no error, against the man who has failed properly to execute his first three shots.

Looking at this new scoring suggestion for the putter, in connection with the new one-half stroke par solution, would not the true value for putter and par be greatly benefitted if both new systems were combined and used together?

Let us make a tentative schedule of pars, using the half strokes, and see how this would work out with the value of each putt at one half a stroke.

Up to 250 yards, par would be 2, one stroke and two putts. From 251 to 300 yards (although this might possibly be extended a little) par would be $2\frac{1}{2}$, two strokes and one putt; and would not perfect play require a second shot which was dead to the pin on a hole of this short length, because such shot would only be of 50 yards, for the drive goes 250 yards under the old system? From 301 to 445 yards, par 3—there would be no argument about this—two strokes to the green, and two putts. From 446 to 500 yards, par would be $3\frac{1}{2}$, and again a short third shot to the green would be required to be dead; and the man who could secure a distance of over the allotted 446 yards, and reach the green in two strokes, would be able, if he

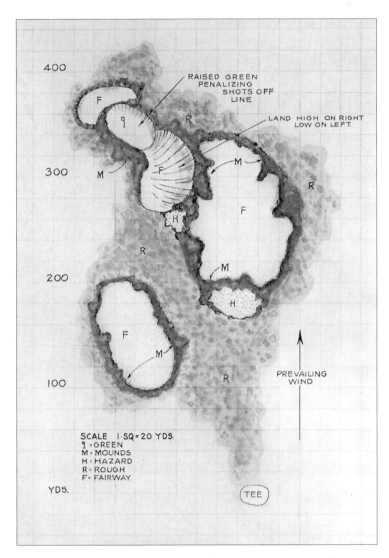

Under present values type of hole which allows a par by short player with two indifferent shots, and gives a very easy second to long hitter. Green too large for perfect play for pars, but mounds and rough dividing fairways improve holes of this class.

If green is made smaller and slope aiding short man eliminated hole too difficult for him. This hole would play better under suggested values without necessity of raising green. (From original drawing.)

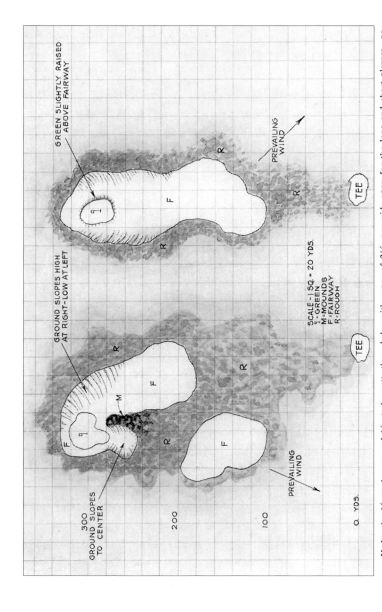

GREEN SLIGHTLY RAISED
ABOVE FAIRWAY

GROUND SLOPES HIGH
AT RIGHT-LOW AT LEFT

GROUND SLOPES
TO CENTER

PREVAILING
WIND

PREVAILING
WIND

SCALE-1 SQ.= 20 YDS.
⬚ = GREEN
M=MOUNDS
F=FAIRWAY
R=ROUGH

TEE

TEE

300

200

100

O. YDS.

Under the ½ stroke par and ½ stroke putt, these holes with a par of 2½, are wide open for the long and short players—no hazards are required, yet it is difficult for the long man to secure par and very hard for the short player to do so. Par requires perfect play but punishing hazards are not necessary. If desired, traps may be added for carries. (From original drawing.)

went down in two putts, to get a birdie 3, under par. Would he not be entitled to this because he had made two superlative shots, the second of which should not be required to be very near the flag? If he went down in two putts he would have made a very fine approach putt, or a very good holing putt. In other words, he would have made three superlative shots out of a possible four. Above 500 yards, and up to 600, the par would be 4, three shots to the green, and two putts; and if advisable, anything over 600 yards may be made 4½ or 5, depending on the distance, although this would seldom be used.

Most certainly, by using the half stroke system for both putts and pars a more honest par would be given, and the putter would be reduced in importance.

It would appear that a good argument in favor of this combined system is the requirement of but one putt when the shot to the green is a very short one on holes between 250 and 300 yards (or possibly slightly longer) because, while 250 yards is the distance required for drives from the tee, nevertheless, many drives are hit considerably further than that. In addition, holes under 300 yards would have even shorter second shots. Should not perfect play demand that such a stroke be near enough for the holing of a putt? The same argument applies to the short third on a 3½ par.

In any event, would this not be a fairer schedule than the scheme of two putts for a par, no matter what the length of the green approach, because, under the present method where a man has to play a shot of close to 200 yards to the green, he is required to go down in two putts; and he is given two putts where he makes a 10 yard approach? This does not seem an equitable arrangement.

This suggestion would make our present weakest holes, those of from 251 to 300 yards, very different propositions for the long man's pars; and what is still more important—in fact, of vital consequence—to golf architecture, it would enable us to build greens on those holes, which the short man, and even the very short players, would be able to reach and hold in two strokes, because we could make the greens larger, and trapping less difficult.

Furthermore, the type of hole which is from 446 to 500 yards would not give a par for five strokes, as under the present scoring. The man who reaches a hole of 446 yards, under ordinary circumstances, in three strokes, has not played three perfect shots or anything like them. If he is a short man and it takes him three full strokes to get there, he has not played up to par. If he is a long man he may miss either his first or his second shot, and is, as a general rule, enabled rather easily to reach the green on his third shot, which is not perfect golf. Under these conditions, par 5 does not in any way represent exceptionally fine effort; whereas, under the new system, the par on such a hole is $3\frac{1}{2}$, which means that the short or wild man, who takes three strokes to reach a green, must go down in one putt to secure par; while the long man who reaches the green in two superlative efforts is given a

Photograph by Rau.

EIGHTH, 303 YARDS, PINE VALLEY, N. J.

(Crump and Colt.)

A fine and very exacting hole for the long player, giving proper value for his par. Too hard for the short and average golfer, who has little chance of holding the green on his second shot. This hole is a very good illustration of the fact that short two shotters, if made sufficiently difficult for the long man, cause unfair hardship to other classes of players.

birdie, if he holes in two putts, and allowed three putts where he may be a hundred feet from the flag.

However, the greatest improvement to be derived from the suggested method would come to the average player, and the help given him will not affect the playing of our best golfers.

This arrangement would increase the size of greens on all short two shotters and short three shotters. There would be fewer traps for the short player to recover from, especially near the green, and yet the long man would be required to play superlative golf to get his pars. Further, carrying traps would not be as necessary on short holes, which would obviate the building of many of them; and the short man would avoid sand without being able, as a rule, to secure pars by inferior shots.

Incidentally, the cost of construction and upkeep would be reduced by the new combined method of one-half stroke putting and one-half stroke pars, and the congestion of courses materially decreased.

Except where the ground is flat, it has generally been found advisable in course construction to use certain contours as units for the proposed holes. Very often it is impossible to do anything else, and after such selection one frequently finds an unused distance of from 250 to 300 yards between the units already provided for. Many times there are contours of this short two-shot hole distance of 250 to 300 yards, which must be used by themselves.

The same situation will be found to apply for short three-shot holes.

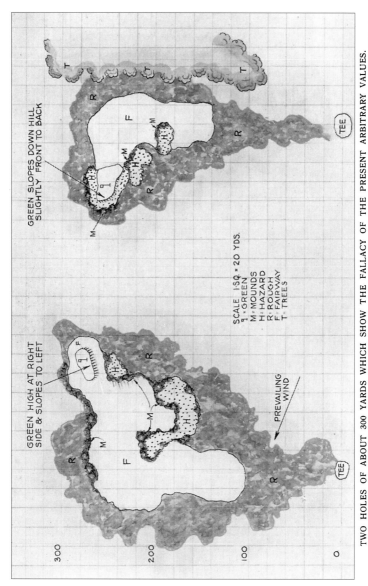

GREEN HIGH AT RIGHT
SIDE & SLOPES TO LEFT

GREEN SLOPES DOWN HILL
SLIGHTLY FRONT TO BACK

PREVAILING
WIND

300

200

100

0

TEE

TEE

SCALE 1 SQ. = 20 YDS.
g = GREEN
M = MOUNDS
H = HAZARD
R = ROUGH
F = FAIRWAY
T = TREES

TWO HOLES OF ABOUT 300 YARDS WHICH SHOW THE FALLACY OF THE PRESENT ARBITRARY VALUES.

At the left, an approximate sketch of No. 10, Los Angeles Athletic; the green is raised above fairway and is extremely difficult for the short man to hold; but he has no punishing hazards. The long hitter, by carrying the optional hazard, has too easy a par or chance at a "birdie." At the right, an approximate sketch of No. 12, Pine Valley, which is a fine test but a punishing hole for the average golfer who cannot carry the optional trap or by going around it secure a running shot to green. The Pine Valley hole demands finer play for a par. The Athletic Club hole is better adapted to a crowded course. In both cases it was impossible to secure balance for all golfers with existing standards.

Every time that holes of these distances are constructed there is disagreement as to their suitability for the long man or for the short man, as it is very difficult with the present arbitrary values to construct these holes for more than one type of player.

In addition to this, under the present scoring, on short three-shot holes, or long two shotters, there is the further argument as to the correct par of the hole. It is hard to decide whether it should be a four or a five, and no matter which is chosen, the selection will be a poor par for one class of player.

Is there a reason why values for play should not be scheduled so that the hole of any length will be a fair test for all golfers in comparison with par?

In recapitulation, we have the following apparent inaccuracies in our present arbitrary values:

1. The putting stroke has too high a value, being 50 per cent of the shots of all clubs in a par of 72 strokes.

2. Our par value, which is supposedly for perfect play, varies in its worth on different holes. It varies so much that it allows three mediocre strokes and two putts, generally of reasonable length, to score perfect play on one hole, while insisting on two extremely difficult strokes, and usually two difficult putts for perfect play on a second hole, with some equally remarkable discrepancies in other situations.

3. To follow our present system, it is nearly impossible on short two shot, or short three-shot holes to arrange a proper test for both the long

and the short players. The result is either an absurdly easy par for the long man, or too hard a proposition for the short golfer.

4. On account of our arbitrary values, it is customary to trap our courses in order to secure them, and this results in unfair hardships to the short players; and there is continued argument on many holes as to the correct placing of traps.

5. By reason of multitudes of artificial hazards, the courses are too greatly congested. One foursome, or group of players, are forced to wait while those in advance recover from sand traps. Under the new scoring suggested, there will be fewer traps, and, therefore, much less congestion, without in any way affecting the quality of play as compared to the right balance of par.

6. In order to make the shot to the green of sufficient difficulty for the long player, it is often necessary to restrict the size of the putting surface. Such greens are difficult for the short player to attain, and on account of their small size, there is not enough room to change the cup correctly, and golfers are often forced, in approach putts, or even in holing putts, to play over a place where the former cup has been located. Under the new system of scoring greens would be made as large as traffic required on all holes, which would enable one part of the green to be rested or improved

Courtesy of Canadian Golfer.

SEVENTH, VICTORIA GOLF CLUB, OAK BAY, VICTORIA, B. C.

while the other is in play, and would obviate the errors just noted.

7. The fact that we would build few hazards would save money in original construction and in cost of upkeep.

8. As a conclusion, golf architecture would have a problem to deal with in which the values provided would make for more common sense courses, without undue penalties for the average golfer. This average golfer is the man who supports the game, and he must be considered. On the other hand, the good golfer and the improvement of our young players should have equally important consideration. Under our present method it is difficult to cater to both of these most desirable objectives. Under the new arrangement we can not only demand of our good golfers more superlative play in order to secure pars, but also render our courses more playable and more pleasurable for the average army of golfers.

As noted in the foreword, this chapter is treated as a separate problem, but the strategy of golf construction would be ill served if its defects were not pointed out as well as its merits, and remedies suggested.

XII

THE UNKNOWN EQUATION

IN THE foregoing chapters the known quantities of Strategy and Construction have been considered. The only factor for which we cannot provide and the cause of many arguments is the golf ball itself. Everyone knows its evolution and how it has been improved in balance, durability and distance getting. At present we have a standardized ball with a specified size and weight, and it would not seem likely that with such restrictions it could be changed very greatly in playing value; yet the unexpected often happens.

Even though the present ball may not be improved by different construction, many persons desire one which they deem better for the game, and this question has been the cause of much comment. A lighter, larger ball which would float is the suggested change.

As the ball makers improved their models, many older courses were too short for the longer flying productions, and the new distances obtained altered golf architecture. Our governing bodies wisely adopted a common standard to prevent further variation. Nevertheless many people believe that a somewhat larger and lighter ball would tend to improve the game.

The present ball sinks in water; its size and weight give it an advantage in playing against the wind over a floater of larger size. It runs through hazards better

Courtesy of William Watson.   SEVENTH GREEN, LAKE ARROWHEAD (5,000 FEET ELEVATION), CALIFORNIA.   *(Watson.)*

Sunlight and shadows coupled with variation of growth and foliage make this green stand out. The fairway narrows at the entrance.

than the other type, and with it a long hitter can secure greater distance. These characteristics are nearly self-evident. It does not take cut as easily as the lighter sphere, and it runs further on the ground, and possibly holds its line better there, as in the air. It is harder to lift out of cuppy lies on account of its greater weight and smaller size; yet even short drivers secure a trifle more length with it. The very hard hitter obtains a greater advantage over the lighter hitter than with the floating type.

Where one man plays a long iron to the green, and the other a mashie or mashie niblick there is a tremendous advantage to the hard hitter with the present ball, but if instead of 30-40 yards his superiority is reduced to 10 or 20, it means little.

The present ball is the answer to the desire of all golfers for more distance.

It is a question whether the average player would be more benefitted by the slight additional distance gained with the small heavy ball and with its line holding qualities in the air and on the ground, or if he would be better served with a floater which he could get up more easily, and which would hold a green better.

Would the short player be more benefitted by being nearer the long driver off the tee or handicapped because he had a slightly longer shot to the green than if playing the heavy ball?

With the floater the hard hitters would find it more difficult to score. The short hitters would also find it harder to score; but would the average player be benefitted? Undoubtedly the fairly long driver would have a better chance against the hard hitter.

In the writer's opinion it would take more skill to secure par with the floater; but how would a floater affect us in our golf architecture? This is our problem.

We could apply all our rules for the building of courses as at present, provided we allowed for the length and running qualities of the floater.

We could make more forced carries because we would have a more even distribution of drives.

We could make somewhat smaller greens and smaller traps because our lighter, larger ball would remain on green or in trap more readily.

We could decrease the length of our courses and demand more pitch shots with less room for their reception.

We would shorten our holes into a prevailing wind, and upwind we would possibly make wider fairways because our floater would not hold its line so well into the wind as the present ball.

Narrow fairways would cause more trouble than at present.

It would be a question, as always, of gauging what the golfer and the ball would do, and arranging our course values to meet the playing conditions.

XIII

UNDERDRAINAGE

UNDERDRAINAGE for fairways, for traps, and especially for greens, is a most important part of golf construction.

Its proper use is necessary in conjunction with the study of soil moisture. The differences found in soil and in rainfall make this subject very complex, while in districts without summer rain and when it is necessary to give artificial sprinkling to the course, the matter must be handled intelligently.

On well-drained land, especially if the soil is light or sandy, and the subsoil not hard-pan or heavy clay, under drainage is not perhaps obligatory, but even under such conditions there will be places on the course where it will be advantageous, and a green not properly drained will not grow good grass.

The Bulletin of the U. S. G. A. Green Section gives a most careful handling of this subject, and various Engineering and Agricultural Experiment Station Bulletins are very valuable, although farm drainage is different from golf drainage.

The Cleveland District Green Section supplies a correspondence course for greenkeepers which is very thorough; and articles by the Agricultural engineer, Wendell P. Miller, are comprehensive.

It would be advisable for the Committee in charge of construction of any course to take up this subject with their golf architect, and if he is not thoroughly conversant with it, arrangements should be made with experts to work with him.

The various factors entering into this question need expert advice.

"The accompanying diagram shows the plan of drainage on No. 10 green at the Columbus Country

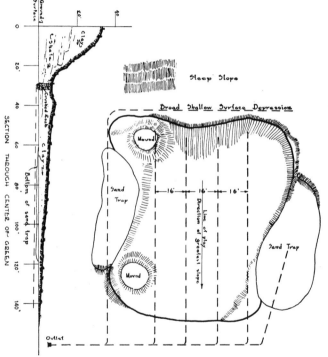

DRAINAGE PLAN OF No. 10 GREEN, COLUMBUS COUNTRY CLUB, COLUMBUS, OHIO.
Drawing by Wendell P. Miller, Drainage Engineer.
Courtesy Bulletin of U. S. G. A., Green Section.

Club. Before installing the shallow surface depression and deep tile ditch at the foot of the hill the green was always soggy and without turf. When the surface of a green is entirely elevated above the surrounding ground and is not subject to seepage water from a hillside, one or two lines of tile installed 2 feet deep in the original subgrade is usually sufficient. Greens subject to seepage or runoff from higher ground should be protected by shallow surface ditches to catch the surface runoff and by tile placed deep enough to intercept the lowest plane of seepage." (Extract from Bulletin U. S. G. A., Green Section.)

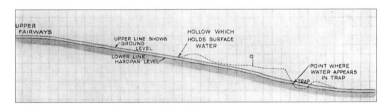

Hard-pan is extremely compact subsoil which nearly stops the downward percolation of water received on the fairway above. Hard-pan usually follows the surface contours, and on a hillside irrigating water will flow downhill underground just above the hard-pan, after percolating through the top soil.

In the illustration the dotted line represents a green built upon a hillside with mound above and trap below. In such a location the irrigation water flows from the upper fairways downhill above and below ground, seeps downward to the hard-pan, runs under the green on the hard-pan, and appears in the trap below.

The only solution is a drain surrounding the green above and slightly below hard-pan, which carries the water past, also tile underdrainage for green.

Beware of traps or greens built below other fairways in a hard-pan country, especially if such go below hard-pan. Protecting underdrainage must be supplied.

"A few maxims of tile drainage are: No tile drain is any better than its outlet. The poorest tile determines the life of the drain—install strong tile. Never install tile less than 30 inches deep unless bedrock or lack of an outlet prevents. Backfill all trenches on the greens, in traps and in fairway depressions, with crushed rock or cinders to within 6 inches of the surface. Make as few connections as possible and make them smooth and tight." (Extract from article by Wendell P. Miller.)

PICTURESQUE PINE VALLEY